The Bear Tribe's
Self-Reliance Book

The Bear Tribe's Self-Reliance Book

Sun Bear, Wabun & Nimimosha

PRENTICE
HALL
PRESS

New York   London   Toronto   Sydney   Tokyo   Singapore

Sections of this book originally appeared in *Many Smokes*, the Native American/Earth Awareness Magazine; and in its successor, *Wildfire*, the Medicine Wheel Network Magazine. The section on Wampanoag Prophecy, which originally appeared in *Many Smokes*, will also be in a forthcoming book by Manitonquat entitled *Return to Creation*.

 Prentice Hall Press
15 Columbus Circle
New York, New York 10023

Published in 1988 by Prentice Hall Press
A Division of Simon & Schuster, Inc.

Originally published in 1977 by Bear Tribe Publishing Co.

PRENTICE HALL PRESS and colophon are registered trademarks of Simon & Schuster, Inc.

Library of Congress Cataloging-in-Publication Data

Sun Bear (Chippewa Indian)
The Bear Tribe's self-reliance book.

Previous ed. entered under title.
1. Indians of North America—Religion and mythology.
2. Home economics—Handbooks, manuals, etc.
3. Agriculture—Handbooks, manuals, etc. I. Wabun.
II. Nimomosha. III. Title.
E98.R3S92 1988 970.004'97 87-47990

ISBN 0-13-071341-4

Manufactured in the United States of America

10 9 8 7 6 5 4

*This book is dedicated to those people
who are striving to be more responsible for themselves
and more responsive to the Earth Mother;
and to Shasta, who taught us so much about love.*

Thanks

We offer thanks to Great Spirit for letting us serve his will.

We offer thanks to Earth Mother for her patience, understanding, perception, acceptance, gentleness, and beauty.

We give thanks to those who have been our teachers, and to those who came to learn, and thus taught us.

We give thanks to our relatives in the mineral, plant, and animal Kingdoms for teaching us, feeding us, and needing our praise.

We offer thanks for this opportunity to share some of the things we've learned.

We thank all those who have ever come to the Tribe for sharing themselves and their learning. We give special thanks to the following people who have put their best love and energy into preparing the first edition of this book: Yarrow McDonald, Ken, Mondamin and Soon-kaax-kwe, Jim, Leon, Mary Kay, Wolf, Barbara, Brad, Carla, Yarrow Goding, Bobby, and Red Bear. We thank Gregory, Stan, and Whispering Leaf for writings they contributed. We thank all of the poets and artists who have contributed work. We thank Bill Durrell and Jean Terra for helping with printing and photo information. We thank those who dropped by and pitched in.

We thank Simon Henderson, with his valuable knowledge and experience in organic gardening, for his help in this revised version of this book, and we thank him for the part he plays in our lives. We thank Cougar for his love of the earth and his insights about acquiring and living on land. We thank Nimimosha. Her growing wisdom and perspective are reflected throughout the book.

We also thank those who are working with the Tribe as this edition is published: Sun Bear, Wabun, Shawnodese, Gaia, Raven, Cougar, Nimimosha, Donna Singing Pipe Woman, Ruth Blue Camas, Casey, Yarrow, Thunderbird Woman, Michelle Odayinquae, Beth Earthseeker, Simon Henderson, Marc Creller, Mary

Fallahay, Matt Ryan, Elisabeth Robinson, Tom Wilson, Saundra Pathweaver, Gail Buckner, and Cheryl Crombie. They, along with many other good people, including Sun Bear's apprentices, have greatly added to our knowledge of self-reliance and of life over these years.

We thank you for buying and reading this book.

Contents

Introduction

If you have ever dreamed of living in the country; if you have ever wondered about joining a community or founding one; if you are one of the millions of people fascinated by the American Indian; if you are a backyard gardener; if you are a person searching for ways to make the world a better place to live; if you are seeking ways to be less wasteful; if you want to find out how to be more self-reliant wherever you are—this book is for you.

The Bear Tribe's Self-Reliance Book gives an overview of all of the topics mentioned above, and more. It will help you to be, or to imagine yourself being, more reliant upon your own skills and knowledge for providing yourself with life's basic necessities. It is an introductory overview for people just beginning to learn self-reliance and a reassuring expression for those who have already begun living with a degree of self-reliance. It is also a book that will help you understand how to nurture the earth and how to affirm life in the way you live each day.

This is not a book of abstract theory. Everything contained within these covers comes from the experience of the authors. Sun Bear, a man of Ojibwa heritage, grew up in the wilds of northern Minnesota. He had to learn how to live with the land and provide for himself in order to survive. He is also a teacher who helps contemporary people understand the Native world view as it relates to life today. He has helped many people find and follow their own path of power.

Nimimosha and I both grew up in the white world, she on a farm in Rhode Island, and I in the survival school of Newark, New Jersey. We both joined Sun Bear and the Bear Tribe because we saw him and his vision as a positive alternative to the world we had known. Together, the three of us have more than fifty years of accumulated experience in community living.

The Bear Tribe is, among many other things, a medicine society of teachers who wish to share with others the knowledge they have gained. This book is full of that knowledge on topics ranging from vision to prophecy to canning food to insurance. There is at least one piece of new knowledge to be gained for every reader of this book.

We do believe that everything you do matters. Each time you treat the Earth with care and sensitivity, she responds. Each time we change our behavior from the old destructive habits we grew up with to new, gentler ways, no matter how small the difference, the Earth responds. The Earth and her children have a remarkable capacity for regeneration, if we will but cooperate fully and from our hearts.

—Wabun

Fable of the Water Clan

—A story shared by Sun Bear

Once upon a time a long time ago some people traveled across the Great Water in canoes that had giant sails upon them. These strange canoes were able to haul the many people coming in search of new land because the rulers in their old lands had become evil and selfish, and had taught the people to hate those who had a different language, or a different way of worshiping the Great Spirit. The rulers encouraged wars that made them profit but caused suffering and death to the people.

When they came to the land of our ancestors our people welcomed them and sat down with them in council and treated them as brothers and sisters. They passed the pipe, smoked, shared good thoughts and words together, and our people and the strangers gave gifts to each other. There was much happiness in the land.

The people who came across the water said they had need of new homes. Our people said, "Come live with us and share our land and our ways and you shall be called people of the Water Clan." The people from across the Great Water looked at the ways of our people and saw that there was peace and plenty and that each man could worship the Great Spirit according to his own vision, so they accepted, with warm gratitude, the offer of our people. The people of the Water Clan learned how to raise crops in the new land, and their sons and daughters married with our people. They learned to respect our system of government where chiefs and counselors sat together and made good decisions for the people.

The Water Clan told horrible tales of other lands where men ruled for money and became corrupt. They said, "This shall not happen here. Our chiefs, like yours, shall counsel for love of the people and they shall work together in the hunt or the fields with their brothers and sisters."

They told other stories of how people were put in prison because they stole when they were hungry, or killed or committed injury against their fellow humans when there were sicknesses in their minds. And they said, "This is bad. It is better if we do as you do and feed the hungry and send people who are sick in these ways to spend time with counselors and medicine chiefs who can help them become well."

As the country grew we founded warm-up centers together where people who felt upset or had problems could go and rest and be warmed up with love from the wise counselors who helped them to expand and find their balance.

As people moved westward they met more tribes of people who had other visions, and they said, "This is the vision for this part of the land. We must respect it. There are different chiefs here and they are loved by their people, so we will accept their knowledge and counsel."

The chiefs there told the people to take of the buffalo only what they needed for food, and the people saw that this was good wisdom that would always leave buffalo for the children yet to come. A chief named Sitting Bull said he had had a bad dream that white men in blue coats came with fire sticks to kill and murder his people. The Water Clan people assured him this would not be, since this was a sickness they had happily left behind when they reached the shores of this new land.

As the Water Clan, along with members of some other clans, moved across the land they continued to meet new people until finally the people knew of each other from sea to sea. In some places people had large villages, but always they raised their food together about the village so that they remembered their balance with the Earth Mother. Each area had a council of chiefs who measured the value of any new ideas according to how they would benefit the people, the Earth Mother, and the Great Spirit.

When a man called Ford discovered an invention that could move people about and cultivate land they said, "This is good if we use it well. We can raise food to feed hungry people in other lands, and we can move necessary items more quickly within our own land. This will enable the people of one area to visit with people from other areas so that we may learn from each other and our hearts may beat more as one." The Water Clan people thought of many inventions that became useful for the good of the people and which worked in harmony with the land, and the other clans said, "It is good that our new brothers and sisters came from across the water to join with us."

When the Water Clan members heard that the people in their old lands had gone crazy and made weapons that killed many people they asked if they might bring these people to the counselors. This was done, and they were placed in warm-up centers until they learned a balance. Then they were sent back to their own lands, and they taught this balance to others while they worked to rebuild the things their madness had destroyed. Certain of our people visited with the traditional leaders in countries even farther to the east, and the chiefs of all the tribes on the planet counseled together and found a way for all the people to live in peace and plenty.

Everyone learned a balance with the Earth Mother, and she became green and bountiful in her joy. The Great Spirit looked to the Earth where all creatures knew their place and purpose and was glad to see their happiness. It is good.

This is how it could have been. This is how it still might be for those people who learn to walk in love and balance on the Earth Mother.

The Bear Tribe's
Self-Reliance Book

I

The Vision

Sun Bear's Vision

The vision is something that is hoped for but not yet seen. The vision is that which leads you on, that which directs you and points the way. The vision is the quest that each young Native man was encouraged to seek, and Native women were free to do so also. In seeking the vision, one would go out and pray, "What shall my purpose be in life, Great Spirit? How can I best serve the needs of my people? What is my part in the universe?" I had my vision when I was very young. With the vision comes the power of direction.

I saw the time when people would come together, when they would learn to live together as brothers and sisters. This would be in a real manner. I saw people living together in groups, sharing and helping each other, Indian and non-Indian alike. I saw the Earth Mother being healed as people began to show real love for the land. But first I saw whole cities become desolate because there was no way left for people to support themselves. I wondered at this when this nation seemed to be all-powerful. Then I saw the vision of the great drought years, a time when the Earth Mother would withhold all increase. I saw great black birds like vultures hovering over withered grain fields, and hungry bands of people traveling across the land in search of food. I knew I must teach people to be self-reliant.

At first, I worked with only Indian people, but in time my work took me to California, and my medicine told me that it was time to start my main work, The Bear Tribe Medicine Society. The vision I had was of people working and sharing together, living on the land, raising their own food, building their own shelters, and at the same time teaching other people the same responsibility to the land, rather than complaining about the things that the overall society does. I would prefer that we teach people how to support their families by living closer to the land, and thereby take away their dependence on city living.

In my vision I saw people returning to the land with a new humbleness and respect for the Earth Mother. I saw new ceremonies coming out of the old. The pipe of peace was there being used in a proper manner, and people came together in an old way that was new again. There was a real sense of sharing. I saw camps of people around natural water, such as rivers, creeks, and springs, working hard to produce their food, but thankful to be alive, for only here and there were small bands of people alive, and they were thankful to the Great Spirit that they were. When people came together they embraced with love, even those who were strangers before that moment, because they knew.

There were only a few people surviving these changes. I've

seen major destruction, and people fleeing great cities, and other people dying from pollution, and cities abandoned, and I wondered why, until these last few years when I see California and other places which no longer have the water, electricity, or natural gases to care for their cities.

Then I understood what I saw before. We were told that our people would lay as if dead in the dust, and then we would rise up on the land again. We were told that the sons and daughters of the possessors of our land would come to us and accept our ways, and that we would live together as one people sharing the land and showing love and understanding for each other.

My medicine directed me to seek out a place that would have a natural water supply. On the Bear Tribe's land we have a spring that supplies our water and needs. It runs out of the mountainside, and there is no need for electric pumps that would stop if there was nothing to power them. We are far enough up the hill that nothing can pollute it, as there is no one above us. Where we lived before, the irrigation district would put a poison in the irrigation ditch to kill the weeds that grew in the ditch, killing off the fish and frogs and polluting the water. We have no dams to burst above us here. We found the pine trees and great rocks of our vision, and so here we live in northeastern Washington. If our vision or medicine told us to move again we would do that, because we cannot be arrogant. We must accept what our vision tells. In the mountains we will hold out our hands and teach and help our fellow beings on the planet earth. It is good to walk in Balance on the Earth Mother.

It gives me great happiness to look at the years since my first vision about harmony with the Earth. It gives me happiness to see that we are living our vision, and that that vision continues to grow, along with our ever-growing awareness. It is a good thing to see the work we did a decade ago remain good, solid, and harmonious while seeing that we didn't stop our sacred journey there, but grew in knowledge. We strive to continue that growth so that the Earth might live.

Medicine Power

In the past, medicine people and societies were an important part of all tribal life. They made medicine and prayers for good crops and for success in the hunt. If the tribe was faced with going to war, the medicine people were consulted. In times of sickness or drought, prayers and ceremonies were made to the Great Spirit.

In the Southwest there are today many kivas and pueblo medicine societies and they function in much the same way as they did in the past. The members go down into their kivas, and the prayers, chants, and medicine made there are known only to them. When the Green Corn ceremony is held in the Pueblo the preparation is first made in the kiva. The Hopi Snake priests make medicine with their people before they dance with the rattlesnakes and ask for rain for their crops. The medicine people are busy as they prepare for the kachina ceremonial. They make prayers asking for the blessing of the Great Spirit on the people.

The individual medicine people today have different medicines they serve. Some work with herbs. They make their prayers and gather herbs to cure those with sickness. Others see with the inner seeing. They search out the future and tell people what is to come in their lives. Others are earth prophets. They ask and seek out what is to happen on the Earth Mother. Others have the responsibility of teaching the old ways. Some use their medicine to help people with alcohol or drug problems.

Medicine, to Indian people, is many things. It can be what is seen through a dream or vision. It can be prayers or herbal knowledge. With true medicine people, each one respects the power or knowledge of the other. No one puts down another or exalts themselves. They feel that each one has something to give to the whole. They do not boast of their power. The doing of the deed is enough in itself.

If a person goes to learn from a teacher, he learns to accept and respect that person's way of teaching. Some people teach by talking and showing. Many watch and listen. And when you can understand and do it, then it's real. Many old medicine people had one apprentice or more, who was there as long as their teacher lived. When the teachers passed on, the apprentices could start practicing the medicine that they had learned. That is part of the reason I have my apprentice program. Spirit told me to pass on my wisdom while I still live so I could be filled with new knowledge.

Today many people are coming alive with the medicine ways. Great Spirit, let it grow, and help them to walk in balance.

Making Good Medicine

Things come about in this way. We see our needs and then make our prayers for good medicine. Each day we work toward our goal and thank the Great Spirit for the gifts of that day. We accept and acknowledge our place in the universe, and we take our responsibility for it.

We know that there are major changes coming on the Earth Mother, and that we should expect them, prepare for them, and accept them. Knowing your place in the universe, and knowing the time of history in which you are living is one way to help your medicine always be good.

Good Medicine is something that should serve you every day of your life. It is not something that you make only on Sunday. In the past our people lived very close to nature. They had a sense of blending and belonging. When they wanted a good corn harvest they made prayers and then worked toward it. The same was true when they went on a buffalo hunt or took care of any other need.

When you move in harmony with the universe and the Earth Mother, then you will have a oneness with all things. Each person, creature, or plant becomes an extension of yourself. When you make prayers or offer the pipe, you offer it for all things, because all things are part of you and your universe. This is why you show respect for all things.

Part of one Ghost Dance prayer is, "When all of the little dreams of horse, buffalo, and man are gone, then we shall be as one." When you feel the true sense of sharing a stream with a fish, or sharing the sky with an eagle, or the land with a prairie dog or deer, then you will not pollute. When people have this respect in their hearts, then their prayers are good and they make good medicine.

For Lack of Love

For lack of love the world died. Today we see the reaping of the harvest. All the selfishness of this nation and all the others is coming to its just reward. Those responsible for taking the natural resources of the earth without concern for future generations; those whose only thought was to make a profit; those responsible for the great wastefulness and destruction of natural resources; and those who murdered people callously will be punished by forces far beyond their reach.

In Asia this nation murdered many of the inhabitants, destroyed their rice fields and rice supplies, and sprayed their lands with chemicals so no food can grow. Americans grew fat from their exploitation of people all over the world, just as, in their earlier days, they stole from the Indians and ignored and mocked their hunger. When they bombed hospitals and murdered people with contract killers, they said, "God is dead, no one will see." But the Great Spirit saw all that happened both in this country and abroad.

While the president of this country paraded himself as the great law-and-order man who said, "We should stop coddling criminals," his own people were busy committing every crime in the book. Then, when he was caught in his lies, he tried to cover them over with other lies. But now, all of his lies and the lies of society are being exposed. How can anyone show love or patriotism for this country? The unions strike and struggle with each other for more money, while big business increases prices. Wherever we look we see greed masquerading as love and concern.

How long will your policemen and firemen be there? Just as long as there is a paycheck in it for them. They have already developed what is called "blue flu" in most big cities. They stay home if their wage demands are not met. The truck drivers will stop hauling to the cities if there's no money involved.

The energy crisis and other crises already have made many people unemployed. There are major food shortages around the world.

All of this suffering and more yet to come because the majority of the people in the world today have been and continue to be selfish. They show no concern or love for anyone but themselves. We see coming the destruction of the major cities, where people today walk in fear with black pitted against white, middle class against the poor. When the transportation system breaks down completely there will be no food in the cities and hungry street gangs will wander, looting and worse.

Brothers and Sisters, I can give you good advice. Find people who you can love and live with; people who share the same direction. Then prepare food resources. There will be very little wild game or food available when the earth changes increase. In recent years there have been no acorns or pine nuts in many places. There are more deer hunters than deer. The Earth Mother will withhold her increase until after the great cleansing and purification. We will live because we believe our old prophecies, and our faith is in the Great Spirit. We will learn to live in love and harmony upon the land.

Wampanoag Prophecy

Many Native people all over the world have prophecies which predict the earth changes Sun Bear has seen in his visions. The following prophecy was written by Manitonquat, a storyteller and keeper of the lore of the Wampanoag nation. It is a section from his forthcoming book *Return to Creation*.

Take a little journey with me now. Take the magic feather, and we will rise together and soar above the forests here of pine and oak. There is Lake Watuppa where some of my forebears lived, and just above it our Watuppa Wampanoag Reservation, where we have many ceremonies during the year. Beyond is the wide reach of the Taunton River, which our people knew as the Titicut, a major waterway for us, proceeding north from Fall River. We will come down on Assonet Neck that narrows the river a little beyond Assonet Bay. There is a state park with a little building that houses and protects a large rock.

This is known as Dighton Rock. There are marks carved all over one side, the side that faces the river. There are many theories about these petroglyphs saying that they were made by Vikings, Portuguese explorers, even Egyptians. There are scores of theories. Of course, our people all know they were made by our ancestors, but theories seem to keep the scholars and hobbyists happy, so we let them alone. They never ask us anyway.

There have been additions over the years, but the basic message was set into the rock a long time ago by a prophet of our people. His name was Weetucks.

At that time, it is said, our people had begun to fall away from the Original Instructions explained to them by Maushop. Maushop had departed many milleniums before. He had come to feel that the people depended on him too much and he was impeding their growth. So he called them together and told them they must assume responsibility for each other, and for the Earth Mother, and

9

all their relatives, the Children of the Earth. Then he went away toward the rising sun, there to remain until the world's end. Some of our people feel that end is soon to come.

After many thousands of years the people had become weak and confused because they neglected the ceremonies that Maushop had taught them, to remind them of their responsibilities toward all of Creation. They had forgotten all about Pesuponk, the sweat lodge. The people were quarreling again, and seeking magic because they were afraid. They forgot to care for each other and to share what they had.

There was a young widow who became pregnant and would not say who the father was. People thought he might be a magician or a demon, and they shunned her. She lived in the forest, some distance from the village, and kept to herself. When the baby was born it was a boy, and she called him Weetucks. Weetucks grew very quickly and soon was helping his mother, hunting and fishing and tending the garden.

When Weetucks was about twelve years old and coming of age, he told his mother that it was time for him to seclude himself alone for a while in the traditional way. She did not know how he knew this, for he never went into the village or talked to anyone, and anyway, the people had all forgotten about such ways.

He was gone for the turning of a moon. People thought he was lost or hurt and searched for him. When he returned he went straight into the village and collapsed on the water path. He was covered with dirt, for he had buried himself in the earth to receive knowledge from the Mother. And he had been on a mountaintop to receive knowledge from Father Sky and from Grandfather Sun, from the winds and the distant stars.

When the village people saw Weetucks covered with dirt, they knew that he had been given his direction on the medicine path. For they remembered that to go back that way into the heart of the Mother and receive her teachings was the traditional beginning of such a journey. When this occurred with no instruction from an elder it meant that the knowledge came directly from Kiehtan, from the Creation itself.

So they knew this boy must have special knowledge, and when he spoke they came and listened. He spoke of the Old Ways, though he had been taught them by no man or woman. He taught them about the Original Instructions of the Creator. He spoke of Maushop's teachings, of the ceremonies that had been forgotten and how they should be done. He showed them again how to heal themselves in the sweat lodge and mud-bath ceremonies, of healing herbs and other knowledge. Some of these things are well known now, and others are closely guarded secrets to be known and used in a sacred manner only by our medicine people.

He was visited one night by two spirit guides from the place of the departed ones, who came to take his mother back on the starpath to the Southwestern Heavens. At that time they spoke to him of the things that would happen to the land and her people. At midsummer the Turkey People to the west came to hear the marvelous boy, who was thought to be a son of Kishtannit. At that time Weetucks told all the people of the prophecies. He said that Hobomocko's whisper of fear would one day spread across the world, and it would bring disease, violence, and starvation over all the earth. Many would die in confusion and ignorance, but those who remembered the sacred teaching, the Original Instructions, would be able to save their children and heal the earth. Many would lose their way, take a wrong turn, leave the sacred path; yet they would still be able, if they understood in time, to retrace their steps and return to the way of Creation, a world of people guided only by their hearts, by love and joy and beauty.

He showed the people the rock on which he had carved the story of the Great Spirit creating and giving instructions to all beings. On the right side are two human beings at the culmination of Creation, one listening and returning upon the Sacred Path, and the other preparing to continue on a path that leads to his own destruction.

This was the last message of Weetucks. Since the Turkey People had long been enemies, there was a great feast in Montaup Village to celebrate this new peace and understanding. It lasted all through the night with much rejoicing and much merriment. Before dawn the people followed Weetucks to the shores of the Turkey Bay where he bade them farewell. As the sun rose behind them, Weetucks walked across the waves toward the Western Heavens and was never seen again.

This is what the carvings on Dighton Rock are really about, unknown to all the scholars and archeologists. That is not all of the message of the rock, but it is not time to reveal more. I am instructed to tell this part of the prophecy now, as it is in keeping with other prophecies of the people of Turtle Island, such as the Hopi message of the Great Purification, the Lakota story of the Great Buffalo, and the Anishnabe prophecies of the Seven Fires.

These prophecies are being told now because it is believed that some will hear and heed. Some from every race and nation will begin to retrace their footsteps and find the sacred path again.

For any of you who may find it hard to believe such old tales from a people who are strange to you, let me speak only of the report of the Club of Rome. This club comprises scores of the foremost scientists of the world, from every area of learning, who studied the trends of the first six decades of the twentieth century and projected them into the future. This scientific prophecy reads just like our own. Famine, disease, violence, all increasing in our lifetime into the greatest destruction humanity has experienced, more devastating to more people than the fire, the ice, or the floods of the past eras.

But you can be your own prophet. Look at what is happening today in the world all around us. Population is increasing, topsoil is washing away to the sea, water tables are receding and becoming polluted. Famine and starvation grow as more and more of the earth is owned by fewer and fewer people. Fear and mistrust are rising on every hand. Families are breaking up, separation increases, generation gaps widen, children are abandoned, abused, neglected. The courts and prisons cannot keep up with the rising rate of crime, which is becoming more and more violent. Terrorism is the political mode of the times, between nations, races, religions, and political factions. Terror stalks the streets of the major cities of the civilized world.

You don't have to be a scientist or a visionary to see where all of this must inevitably lead. No one who has the public's attention, no political leader, no voice of authority and respect has put forward any workable solutions to all of this.

Under these conditions I do not find it strange that there is such apathy and frustration, such hopelessness and barely suppressed anger among people today. I do not find it surprising that young people turn to drugs or cults or the immediate thrill of sensual pleasures. It is hard to rally folks to a good cause these days. What cause can mean anything in the numbing catastrophes revealed relentlessly in the news media every day of our lives?

Yet wherever I speak, the message I bring is one of hope. The message I bear from prophecy, vision, and instruction by the traditions of my elders is that it is not too late for those who will listen and heed.

Humankind has created all of the problems which it now faces, and humankind can solve them, if it will. The same genius that has created incredible weapons of destruction and has probed beyond the earth to the very stars could certainly find a way to bring the people of earth together for their own survival. But it is as though we were in a burning house, and all the people in it, instead of trying to put out the fire, were just redecorating their rooms and stealing from the house and one another to do it.

There is no doubt in my mind that millions of people will not be able to survive the holocaust that we are even now preparing for ourselves. There is also no doubt in my heart that those who find again the sacred path of the Creator will survive and create a society of harmony and joy, wiser and stronger for the lessons of this age of terror and ignorance.

It is hard, in a world that already has so much suffering in it, to think that it will soon be worse beyond our imagining. But because it is hard we should not refuse to see it, to look at it, think about it, and to take action in our lives.

People speak of political problems, economic problems, sociological problems, psychological problems, and everyone has a pet theory of how to solve his or her own pet problem. These are only little bandages on the sores of a diseased body. A deeper remedy must be found for the inner cause of the disease.

At the deepest level, the disease is spiritual. The problems are all spiritual. Spirituality, as I conceive it, is simply the relationship of all things in the universe. Instead of thinking only of ourselves, we must consider our families, our children, our unborn generations, our planet and all the beings who share it with us, all the stars and beings in all of the cosmos, and that One that has made it all.

Where it must begin is with *trust*. Unless we trust that the Creation is good, that it works, that we are good, that we can learn to live in a good way in this Creation, then we give ourselves over to despair. Once we have this trust, we need only to discover the way that Creation works, find the path, and follow it. Fortunately we have many guides who have followed that path before us and many who are following it now. And we have the guide of the heart within us.

There is an old Indian saying that every step we take upon the earth should be as a prayer. Now, a prayer is just a way of becoming really conscious, really tuning in to all the relationships of everything in existence. To make every step a prayer we simply need to be totally conscious in every act we make. Most of us spend most of our waking hours half asleep, only dimly aware of our feelings, to say nothing of what is going on in the world.

Now let us consider the Original Instructions. Let us begin to retrace our steps and find the Sacred Path again. As we go, let us walk in a sacred manner by letting each step be as a prayer. In this way we will find the Path of Beauty, the Path of the Heart, and return to Creation once more.

Hopi Prophecy

The following Hopi prophecies are largely from messages of the Hopi elders delivered over the past decades. Sun Bear especially thanks his spiritual brother, Soloho, who is now in the spirit world, for all of the information he gave him on these prophecies.

In the Hopi religion, the name applied to the Creative Force is Taiowa (The Infinite). This Force, in the Beginning, conceived of the individual Sotuknang (The Finite) and commanded him to create "Lesser Beings." Sotuknang created the twins, Poqanghoya (North Pole) and Palonqawhoya (South Pole). He also created Kokyangwuti (Spider Woman). She created man out of earth that was in four colors: Yellow, Red, White, and Black. Another tool used in the creation of man was tuchvala (saliva). Over her creations she spread the Cloak of Creative Wisdom and breathed life into them.

There were three phases of Creation at the Dawn of Creation. The first phase is the Time of the Dark Purple Light, known as Quganguptu. Here was the basic physical creation without life. Only the physical forms were established—there was, as yet, no life.

The second phase is the Time of the Yellow Light, known as Sikangnuya. Here the Breath of life was introduced into these physical forms.

The third phase is the Time of the Red Light, known as Talawva. Here the life forms were fully completed and began to develop.

The People have lived, since the Dawn of Creation, on Four Worlds. The First World was *Tokpela* (Endless Space). The direction is considered to be West, and the color associated with the world is Sikyangpu (Yellow). The mineral related to Tokpela is Sikyasvu (Gold), and the chief life forms were Katoya (The Great Headed Snake), Wisuko (Bird Who Eats Fat), and Muha (The Plant With Four Leaves). This World was lived upon by the People for quite some time until they began to lose sight of their origin. They lost the use of the Vibratory Center on the top of the head (Kopave), and the Soft Spot that was the doorway between the body and the spirit began to harden. Taiowa decided that would never do, and so he ordered Sotuknang to destroy the world, but to save a few people from destruction. He led them into the center of the World where they were received by the Ant People. The Ant People fed them so well that they, themselves, began to grow thin. It is said that this is the reason why today the Ant People have such thin waists. As the People stayed underground, the volcanoes on the surface of the First World erupted, and the whole World caught fire. After the fires subsided, the People came up from their shelter and began to move to the Second World that had been prepared for them.

The Second World was called *Tokpa* (Dark Midnight). The direction is considered to be South, and the color, blue. The related mineral was Qochasiva (Silver), and the chief life forms were Salave (Spruce), Kwahu (Eagle), and Kolichigan (Skunk). Here again, the People lived until they forgot their origin and grew cold and hard to the ways of the Good Life. And so, once again, Sotuknang was ordered to destroy the World. This time, he ordered the Twins, Poqanghoya and Palongawhova, to leave their stations at the North and South Poles and let the World be destroyed. They did this, after the People had once again hidden with the Ant People underground. After the twins left their stations the world's stability was removed, and so it flipped end over end and everything on it was destroyed by ice. The World froze over completely. In this legend we see evidence of two ideas now held by scientists: Polar Reversals and the Glaciation of the last Ice Age. After the ice had melted enough to make the World inhabitable, the People came up from their shelter and began to move into the Third World.

The Third World was called *Kuzkurza* (a word for which it is said there is no modern meaning). The direction is considered to be East, the color red. The related mineral was Palasiva (Copper) and the chief life forms were the Piva (Tobacco), Aungwusi (Raven), and Chuvio (Antelope). Here the People established great cities and a great technology. Much of what is considered to be modern inventions were in use there, such as airplanes. The People, however, lost sight once again of their origin and that which had been taught to them at the time of their creation. They flew in the flying machines, called Patowavta, to other cities and there attacked them at night when they could not be seen. Such evil things as war and the establishment of boundaries and fences came into being. Again, the People turned evil and Taiowa ordered the destruction of the Third World. This time the Chosen People were sealed into hollow tubes and set to float upon the water, for the World was to be destroyed by water. Legend says that the waves grew taller and taller and eventually began to sweep over the land—they are said to have been higher than the mountains.

Before that happened the Faithful ones asked and received permission from the Great Spirit to live with Him in this new land. Great Spirit said, "It is up to you. If you are willing to live according to my Teachings and Instructions and will never lose faith in the life I shall give you, you may come and live with me." The Hopi and all who were saved from the great flood made a Sacred Covenant with the Great Spirit. They made an oath that they will never turn away from him.

The Fourth World, known as *Tuwaquachi* (World Made Complete) is considered to be in the direction North. The color is Sikyangpu (yellow, nearly white). The related mineral is Sikyapala (many minerals mixed) and the chief life forms are Tohopko (Puma), Kneumapee (Juniper), and Mongwau (Owl, Sacred Messenger). This is the present world where the Hopi live now.

The prophecies of the destruction of this world and the inevitable move to a Fifth World are numerous. They concern the idea that the Fourth World may be destroyed by radiation and that the People will, once again, have to hide underground. Again, there will be a Chosen Few, those who are ready and willing to receive the Truth once again. They say that the northern part of Arizona and New Mexico will be relatively safe from harm. The prophecies say that those who knew the truth in the ancient land (for example Europeans, Africans, and East Asians) will be the instrument for the destruction of this World with their radioactivity. So far, history seems to be going along with the Hopi prophecies very well—not to mention the prophecies of other people that agree with the Hopi independently. Mankind continues to put more and more radiation into the atmosphere and he forgets more and more about the Brotherhood of Life, to which he is not a superior member but an equal brother to all. He begins to lose sight of the fact that the Earth is Mother.

To the Hopi, the Great Spirit is *all* powerful. He appeared to the first people and taught them how to live, to worship. In order to safeguard his land and life He made a set of Sacred Stone Tablets into which he breathed all teachings, instructions, prophecies, and warnings. Before the Great Spirit hid himself He placed before the leaders of different groups different colors and sizes of corn for them to choose which shall be their food in this world. Hopi waited last and picked up the smallest one. By this means, Hopi showed himself to the Great Spirit as intelligent. The Great Spirit said that he had done well, obtaining the real corn while the others got imitations, inside of which were hidden seeds of different plants. Because of this, the Great Spirit placed in his hands the Stone Tablets, Tiponi, symbol of power and authority over all land and life, to guard, protect, and hold in trust for the Great Spirit until he returns in later days.

The Chief who led the Faithful Ones to this new land and life fell into evil ways and died. His two sons, brothers of the same mother, scolded their father for the mistake he had made and, after he died, they took over the responsibilities of Leadership. To these two brothers a set of Sacred Stone Tablets were given, and both were instructed to carry them to a place to which the Great Spirit had guided them. The Older Brother was to go immediately to the East, to the Rising, and upon reaching his destination was to immediately start back to look for his younger brother who remained in the land of the Great Spirit. His mission was to help his younger brother bring about Purification Day, at which time all wicked or wrongdoers shall be punished or destroyed, after which real peace, brotherhood, and everlasting life shall be brought about. He'll restore to his brother the land that the Evil One among white man shall have taken from him. He will also come to look for the Sacred Stone Tablets and to fulfill the Sacred Mission given him by the Great Spirit.

The Younger Brother was instructed to cover all land, to mark well his footprints as he goes about in this land. Both of the Brothers were told that a great White Star would appear in the sky as the people moved about in this land and in other lands. They were told that when that happened *all* people shall know that Older Brother has reached his destination, and thereupon all people were to settle wherever they may be at that time, until the Older Brother returned to him. It is said that the Older Brother, after many years, may change in color of skin, which may become white, but his hair will remain black. He will also have the ability to write things down and will be the only one to read the Sacred Stone Tablets. When he returns to this land and finds his younger brother these Stone Tablets will be placed side by side to show all the world that they are *True Brothers*.

In ancient times it was prophesied by our forefathers that this land would be occupied by the Original Peoples, who have received permission from the Great Spirit Massau'u, and then from another land a white brother would come, supposedly to help his brothers who are here taking care of the land and life in a spiritual way with prayer, ceremonies, and humility. He would come either with a strong faith and righteous religion which Massau'u had given him, or he would come after he had abandoned the great life plan and fallen to a faith of his own personal ideas which he invented before coming here. It was known that the white man is an intelligent person, an inventor of many words and material things, a man who knows how to influence people because of his sweet way of talking. He would use many of these things upon us when he came. The white brother would do many things that will be good for our Native Brother.

When it becomes the sole purpose of getting control of this land and he lives only for his own self-glory, then we must not listen to his sweet tongue, but watch his deeds. If he mistreats us, lies, and starts to force our people off their lands, we must wait for our true brother who has the other set of sacred stone tablets.

The Hopi has not listened to the first white brother. We Hopi have been faithful to the instructions of the Great Spirit, Massau'u, up to this time. We have followed our life plan. We are still carrying on our sacred rites and ceremonies—we are still living in accordance with the pattern of life Massau'u has given us. We have not lost our faith in Massau'u. He has given us many prophecies. He told us the white brother would come and be a very intelligent man, bringing to us many things he would invent. One invention that our forefathers spoke of was a machine, or object, that would move on the land with animals pulling it—the wagon. Our forefathers also talked of a machine which would afterwards move with nothing pulling it—when we saw the automobile we understood. Then they said that the land would be cut up and that there would be many roads. Today we see pavement all over the land. Later there would even be roads in the sky, where people will travel. Now we see airplanes. It was said by Massau'u that if and when a gourd of ashes is dropped upon the earth that many men will die, and that the end of the materialistic way of life is near at hand. We interpret this as the dropping of atomic bombs on Hiroshima and Nagasaki. We do not want to see this happen again, here or any place on our Earth Mother. Instead, we should now turn all this energy for peaceful uses, not for war.

The white brother, up to the present time, through his insensitivity to the way of nature, has desecrated the face of Mother Earth. The white brother's advanced technological capacity has occurred as a result of his lack of regard for the spiritual path and for the way of all living things. The white brother's desire for material possessions and power has blinded him to the pain he has caused Mother Earth by his quest for what he calls natural resources. And the path of Massau'u has become difficult to see by almost all men, even by Native First People who have been forced into white brothers educational systems and now have chosen to follow the path of the white brother. We are coming to the time of the purifiers, who were commissioned by the Great Spirit to stop man's destruction of self and nature.

It is known that our True White Brother, when he comes, will be all-powerful and he will wear a red cap or red cloak. He will be large in population and belong to no religion but his very own. He will bring with him the Sacred Stone Tablets. Great will be his coming. None will be able to stand against him. All power in this world will be placed in his hand, and he will come swiftly, and in one day get control of this whole continent. Hopi has been warned never to take up arms.

With him there will be Two Great Ones, both very intelligent and powerful, one of which will have a symbol or sign 卐 which represents purity and is a male. Also ✖ which represents purity and is a female, a producer of life. It is also known that he will wear a cap similar to the Horned Toad ⌒. The third or second one of the helpers to our True White Brother will have a sign or a symbol of Sun ☼. He too will be many people, and very intelligent and powerful.

The Hopis say that these signs together represent the world, and that when the time of Purification Day is near, those with these signs will shake the earth two times. Then it will fall upon the Third One, with whom these two will join together, and they will come as One to bring on Purification Day and to help the younger brother who waits in this land.

It is also prophesied that if these three fail to fulfill their mission, then the *one* from the West will come like a big storm. He will be many, many people, and unmerciful. When he comes he will cover the land like ants. The Hopi people have been warned not to get up on house tops to watch as he will come to punish all people.

Then if none of these fulfill their mission in this life the Hopi leaders will place their prayer feathers to the four corners of the earth in an appeal to the Great Spirit. He will cause lightning to strike the Earth People. Only the righteous ones will revive. Then if all people turn away from the Great Spirit he will cause the great waters to cover the earth again. We humans shall have lost the chance to enter Everlasting Life. They say the *ants* may inhabit the earth after that.

But if the *three* fulfill their sacred mission, and if One or Two or Three Hopi remained fast to the last on these Ancient Teachings or Instructions, then the Great Spirit, Massau'u, will appear before all that will be saved, and the *three* will lay out a new life plan that leads to Everlasting Life. This earth will become new as it was from the beginning. Flowers will bloom again, wild game will come home, and there will be abundance of food for all. Those who are saved will share everything equally. They will all recognize the Great Spirit, and they may intermarry and may speak *one tongue*. A new religion will be set up if the people desire it.

Today, almost all the prophecies have come to pass. Great roads like rivers pass across the landscape; man talks to man through the cobwebs of telephone lines; man travels along the roads in the sky in his airplanes; two great wars have been waged by those bearing the Swastika and the sun symbol; as prophesied by our Religious Elders, man is tampering with the moon and the stars. Hopi and other Native Brothers were warned no man should bring anything down to earth from the moon. It will create unbalance of natural and universal laws and create more severe earthquakes, floods, hail storms, seasonal changes, and famines. This is now happening. Most men have strayed from their life plan shown them by Massau'u. These signs tell us we are nearing the end of our life patterns.

This is what the Hopi know and wait for by adhering to their way of life, and in spite of hardship, they have been faithful up to this day. For they are upholding this land and life for all Righteous people.

Iroquois Prophecy

The following prophecy, attributed to Deganawida, the prophet of the Iroquois people, was related by the late Mad Bear Anderson, an Iroquois medicine person.

When Deganawida was leaving the Indians in the Bay of Quinte in Ontario, he told the Indian people that they would face a time of great suffering. They would distrust their leaders and the principles of peace of the League. A great white serpent was to come upon the Iroquois that, for a time, would intermingle with the Indian people and would be accepted by the Indians, who would treat the serpent as a friend. This serpent would in time become so powerful that it would attempt to destroy the Indian, and the serpent is described as choking the life's blood out of the Indian people. Deganawida told the Indians that they would be in such a terrible state at this point that all hope would seem to be lost. He told them that when things looked their darkest a red serpent would come from the north and approach the white serpent, which would be terrified. Upon seeing the red serpent, he would release the Indian, who would fall to the ground almost like a helpless child, and the white serpent would turn all its attention to the red serpent.

The bewilderment would cause the white serpent to accept the red serpent momentarily. The white serpent would be stunned and take part of the red serpent and accept him. Then there would be a heated argument and fight. Then the Indian revives and crawls toward the land of the hilly country, where he assembles his people together, and they renew their faith and the principles of peace that Deganawida had established. There would be at the time, among the Indians, a great love and forgiveness for their brothers. In this gathering would come streams from all over—not only the Iroquois but from all over—and they would gather in this hilly country, and would renew their friendship. And they would remain neutral in the fight between the white serpent and the red serpent.

While they are watching the two serpents locked in battle a message comes to them which makes them ever so humble. When they become that humble they are waiting for a young leader, an Indian boy, possibly in his teens, who will be a choice seer. Nobody knows who he is or where he comes from, but he will be given great power, and will be heard by thousands. He will give them guidance and the hope to restrain them from going back to their land and he will be the accepted leader. Deganawida said that they will gather in the land of the hilly country beneath the branches of an elm tree, and they should burn tobacco and call upon Deganawida by name when facing the darkest hours, and he will return.

Deganawida said that as the choice seer speaks to the Indians that number as the blades of grass, being heard by all at the same time, and as they gather watching the fight, they notice from the south a black serpent coming from the sea, and he is described as dripping with salt water. And as he stands there, he rests for a spell to get his breath, all the time watching to the north to the land where the white serpent and the red serpent are fighting. It is said that the battle between the white and the red serpents opened real slow but that it became so violent that the mountains would crack and the rivers would boil and the fish would turn up on their bellies. Then there would be no leaves on the trees in that area, and no grass, and strange bugs and beetles would crawl from the ground and attack both serpents, and a great heat would cause the stench of death to sicken both serpents. Then, as the boy seer is watching this fight, the red serpent reaches around the back of the white serpent and pulls from him a hair, which is carried toward the south by a great wind into the waiting hands of the black serpent. As the black serpent studies this hair it suddenly turns into a woman, a white woman who tells him things that he knows to be true, but he wants to hear them again. When this white woman finishes telling these things, he takes her and gently places her on a rock with great love and respect. And then he becomes infuriated at what he has heard, so he makes a beeline for the north and enters the battle between the red and white serpents with such speed and anger that he defeats the two serpents, who have already been battle weary.

When he finishes, he stands on the chest of the white serpent, and he boasts and puts his chest out like he's the conqueror, and he looks for another serpent to conquer. He looks to the land of the hilly country and then he sees the Indian standing with his arms folded and looking ever so noble so that he knows that this Indian is not the one he should fight. The next direction that he will face will be eastward, and at that time he will be momentarily blinded by a light that is many times brighter than the sun. The light will be coming from the east to the west over the water, and when the black serpent regains his sight he becomes terrified and makes a beeline for the sea. He dips into the sea and swims away in a southerly direction, and shall never be seen again by the Indians. The white serpent revives, and he, too, sees this light and he makes a feeble attempt to gather himself and go toward that light. A portion of the white serpent refuses to remain but instead makes its way toward the land of the hilly country, and there he will join the Indian People with a great love like that of a lost brother. The rest of the white serpent will go to the sea and dip into the sea and be lost out of sight for a spell. Then suddenly the white serpent will appear again on the top of the water and he will be slowly swimming toward the light. Deganawida said that the white serpent would never be a troublesome spot for the Indian people. The red serpent would revive and he would shiver with great fear when he sees that light. He would crawl to the north and leave a bloody shaky trail northward, and he would never be seen again by the Indians. Deganawida said that as this light approaches he would be that light, and he would return to his Indian People. When he returns, the Indian people would be a greater nation than they ever were before.

Other Prophecies

This prophecy was shared by a medicine person who writes under the name "The Sly Ole Fox."

I'm always interested in Indian prophecy, and I learned of one from the Manitoba Indians which I'd like to share with all of you.

It seems that the Indians up there knew about the white man coming to their land, and that he would be like a plague of locusts. Many warnings would be given to the white man to be good to his red brother and our Earth Mother. He would be warned to change his ways, and if he did not change, the Creator would cause many natural catastrophes over which the white man could have no control. Great winds would sweep across the prairies taking everything with them. Nothing would be left standing. The Indian people would band together to help one another. The mountains would have great landslides, and earthquakes would crack the land near the sea. Destruction would be everywhere. The earth would change. Great huge animals would also be returning (a sea serpent has already been seen in one of the lakes). The land of ice and snow would grow warmer, and Greenland would be green again. The Indian people would once more be in control of their country.

While I was in Canada I talked with some Northern Crees and Chippawayans. They said the ice floes are changing, something different is happening to the ice lands. They can't explain it, but a change is happening there.

Makes one think, heh?

This prophecy was shared by Sun Bear.

At night I made my prayers and asked to see what would happen on the Earth Mother. I dreamed I saw hungry groups of people roving in search of food. I saw them in desperation throwing their lives against people who were even armed to try and take food. Then, in their anger, they set fire to the homes and buildings of the people.

I saw people in cities who thought they were safe trapped in concrete vaults, destroyed by great floods of water.

I saw wheat fields being destroyed by rust, and I saw some men deliberately using some kind of deformed plants that spread a sickness. I saw people trying to harvest wheat that was so full of rusty-type sickness that the grains stuck together like syrupy candy. There were crows and vultures sitting together on the rotting crop.

This prophecy comes from a speech of Chief Seattle made in 1855.

> Tribe follows tribe
> And nation follows nation
> Like the waves of the sea.
> It is the order of nations
> And regret is useless.
> Your time of decay may be distant
> But it will surely come.
>
> For even the white man whose God
> Walked and talked with him
> As friend to friend
> Cannot be exempt from the
> Common destiny.
> We may be brothers after all.
> We shall see.

A Gift of the Four Directions

The following poems have been shared with us by Whispering Leaf With Blue Jacket, a Shawnee man who had a traditional camp in Tennessee in the 1970s.

As we once again turn our faces toward the daybreak star, and our fear of the darkness lessens, may the teachings and instructions of Great Spirit illuminate our hearts. This is a time of awakening, and as we pray to Great Spirit for guidance, many sacred ceremonies and traditions are returned to us through dreams and visions. One sacred gift which has been renewed is the medicine or peace shield. Of this gift I would now speak:

The Great Spirit
Sensing much confusion among Earth
   Mother's children as they
   struggled through daily life,
Prepared a special gift.

Taking a rainbow, Great Spirit formed
   it into a blanket and spread it
   upon the breast of Mother Earth.
Then with the whispering of the wind,
And the roar of thunder,
The brightness of the morning star,
And the warmth of the summer's sun,
The clearness of the autumn sky,
And the depth of the great sea,
The suppleness of a spring sapling,
And the strength of the mighty oak,
The vision of the eagle,

And the stamina of the bear,
The wisdom of the ages,
And the great silence of the sky,
With these things,
The Great Spirit created forty-four
  warriors of the rainbow.
To each one,
He gave a special shield,
And because these shields could
  pierce darkness and drive
  fear before them,
They were called sacred medicine
  shields.
Now these forty-four warriors, who
  were called peace chiefs,
Were instructed to ride to the four
  directions and to count coup on
  fear, ignorance, deceit and
  jealousy,
The four warriors of darkness.

Whispering Leaf With Blue Jacket, Blades of Grass, and Butterfly in front of their wegiwa

So even though these peace chiefs carry
  no war lance,
They are easy to recognize;
For besides the special shields,
They wear white buckskins of justice
  through wisdom,
Ride upon golden ponies of truth and
  light,
And smoke the sacred pipe of love and
  understanding.

So now, once again, around small campfires throughout the land the teachings of the sacred medicine shields may be heard. Firelight flickers, and in the dancing light the painted symbols of the medicine shield seemingly come to life. It is a time of renewal, and hearts are filled with new hope and strength.

First let me put a few more sticks upon the fire, and then I will tell you a story of how one of these shields was returned to the people.

Not so many winters ago, a young warrior sought to place his feet upon the good red road. Now his people were few and scattered like leaves before the wind, and many of these had now forgotten the Original Instructions. So, alone with this spiritual hunger, he set out upon his quest. First he traveled toward the setting sun, the place of looks within. As the cold moons were approaching, he made camp in the mountains, and each day he would climb a sacred mountain and ask Moneto, "Who am I?" After many moons of daily climbing the snow-covered mountain to ask his question, Moneto spoke to him. In a soft voice upon the wind came his answer.

"Young warrior, you are a son of Mother Earth and Father Sky and your breath is of the Great Universal Mystery of Creation."

With this new understanding, the young warrior broke camp and resumed his journey. This time he traveled to the north, the place of wisdom. And after making camp, he began to fast and pray.

> Oh Mother Earth
> And Father Sky!
> I pray to Moneto
> Why am I?
> Alone I stand
> Upon holy ground
> On a vision quest
> I am bound!
> Oh spirit of the north
> hear my plea,
> I'm seeking your wisdom
> To truthfully guide me.

And after he had sung this prayer many times to the four directions, he began to notice something about the trees and grasses, the winged and the insects. It seemed as if all of creation was honoring the master of life through song and dance. He watched the trees and grasses sway to and fro as they sang with rustling leaves. The winged would pour forth great song to the rising and setting sun, while insects kept up a steady song day and night. And he began to wonder if perhaps he, too, should not honor this spirit. Then clear and strong came his inner voice speaking to his heart. "Yes, oh child of the Mother Earth and Father Sky, you are alive that you may know, love, and serve the Great Spirit which is in all things and beyond all things."

Having learned this new truth, he once again resumed his journey, this time toward the rising sun, the place of illumination. Finally he reached a very tall mountain, and, climbing to the top, he spread his blanket and sat down. Now he prayed, "Oh Moneto I am of your breath. You have given me life so that I may honor you. How may I best serve your will?"

Now it became night and the sky was filled with clouds and a light rain began to fall. After awhile, Grandmother Moon in all her fullness appeared. She spoke in a gentle voice to the young warrior. "You must make peace with your past, for the path ahead can only be walked in the spirit of life. Chase away all shadows from your heart." Then Grandmother Moon once again hid herself behind the clouds and rain fell as before. At dawn, the warrior descended to the valley so that he might make peace in his heart. And when he had done this, a mockingbird sang to him. The winged messenger instructed this new peace warrior to paint a sacred shield. When it was finished, he was told to carry it to the south so that he might be of service to Moneto.

Thus began the last and longest part of the journey to the place of love and compassion. As he began to walk in this direction many voices tried to lure him astray from his goal. In the night came the voices of fear and doubt urging him to turn back. Oftentimes he would stop and wonder if he was strong enough to continue his journey.

Now we may see how the gift of the medicine shield can be of help. Each time we falter in our journey, a look at our shield reminds us of who we are, why we are, and what our duty is in this life. It erases the seeds of doubt and confusion which are sprouting all around us during these troubled times. The shield reminds us that we seek to become a whole medicine circle and to turn in harmony with the four seasons of life while carrying the gifts of the four directions within our hearts.

When I first received the shield I felt a sense of despair. How was I to revive this medicine that had been lost for one hundred years? Since I could not answer this question, I had to let the breath of Great Spirit guide me. This Whispering Leaf was blown and tossed for many moons until at last he came to rest on a little stream in the hills of central Tennessee. This stream we call Singing Sweetwater Creek, and it is here that a small camp of the medicine shield has been established. With the strength of the medicine shield we have been able to sustain this camp and its traditional way of life.

Living on the barest of subsistence levels, we have been able to call on the help of our ancestors who speak to us through the wind and waters and teach us how to build quonset wigewas, plant corn and beans in small hills, gather and dry herbs for healing, and how to think and act with a family awareness. By this family awareness,

I mean the act of sharing ourselves and our energies with our brothers and sisters so we can all grow in the spirit.

Our time has not been easy in this new camp, as ignorance of the natural world was an obstacle to growth. We had to learn to Walk in Balance with our Mother before she would yield her wisdom and abundance. Through all this, when the doubts and fears and frustrations would attack the heart, it was the strength within the shield that would sustain our effort. It is a constant reminder that we are of the Creation and our sole purpose is to know, love, and serve the Creator. It is this service to Great Spirit in a hostile world that has turned away from the instructions of Creation that makes the journey to the place of love and compassion the longest and most difficult. It is here that the warriors of light with their sacred medicine shields must conquer the fear, ignorance, deceit, and jealousy spread by the warriors of the darkness.

It is a good day to begin the struggle. I have spoken.

Rebirth of the Spirit

These thoughts come from Wabun, one of Sun Bear's medicine helpers.

When we sit quietly to reflect, we all know the feelings the words in this article seek to express. At those times we are free to feel in our hearts our connection to the rest of the circle of the universe. We experience the peace that comes from knowing, as the traditional Indian does, that you are one part of the whole universe, and not *the* whole universe. We know then that the world is flowing, changing as it should, and that we are progressing as we should.

Indian societies were designed to reinforce these feelings at all times. The world was considered sacred—plants, animals, people, and their actions were all sacred. People were taught to respect all things for their implicit, natural beauty and holiness. The world was seen as an ocean of balanced energies, all running along their proper courses.

Sadly, we find little in the daily life of the society built by the people who tried to destroy the religion and culture of the Indian

31

peoples that is designed to allow us to remember that feeling of being one with the world around us. From cradle to casket, competition is stressed. As infants in this society we learn that even love comes with a price tag. We sense that people fussing over us in many cases aren't doing it to make us happy. They're doing it so we'll smile and laugh and make them feel good and look good to others. In a short period of time we learn how to manipulate those around us so we can look good too. Our lifelong affection and approval sweepstakes—that which we usually call love—has begun. We've entered the Great American Rat Race.

By the time that most of us get to school, we're set up for the "socialization" process there. Our already insecure young minds eagerly accept America's golden rule: "He who is on top is best." We begin to shove and push to get to the top: to be first in the class, the teacher's pet, the best athlete, mama's little angel. Always, and in everything—school, family, church, music, television, literature—we are given the message that the winner, automatically, is a good guy, and even more, a person who feels he belongs. Throughout, this emotional message is backed by the economic system which rewards the best competitor. To the victor went the spoils, and few people seemed to care how the victory was won.

Eventually, growing up, some of us began to question whether the end of winning justified all of the dirty means being used. Those of us who had won found that while our image might be improved, we still had no sense of belonging, of contentment. If you were president of the senior class, you really wanted to be president of the student body. And if you were that, you still envied the scholarship to Harvard the president of your rival high school got. Rats on a treadmill, running toward an undefined home.

In the Sixties, when most of us had full bellies, we called time out to look at where we were headed, individually and as a society. Some of us were so disgusted that we followed the lead of a few dissatisfied radicals, bohemians, and utopians of the past and dropped out of playing the game by the rules we had been taught. We formed what was called "The Movement," the "counterculture." This alternate culture was never the unified group that the government's paranoia painted. It was composed of radicals, revolutionaries, rock heads, plain heads, women's libbers, communards, collectivists, and a lot of hangers on, the people so bruised by the battle of life that they seemed unable to ever commit themselves to anything. Being a member of the counterculture was, at first, exciting. Black, white, red, brown, yellow, together we were going to overcome the evil system that discriminated, maimed, and killed to serve its own greed. We demonstrated, sat in, campaigned, debated. Eventually, the excitement ebbed, money dwindled, and we became discouraged. Many of our veterans turned to drugs, a more vicious mind killer than the fears they used them to forget; or to hedonism; or to the system they despised.

Others graduated from the political movement into the communal one. These people said that they felt if they couldn't change the dominant system they could create a viable and pleasant alternative. They felt that if they couldn't change the world for everyone, they could try to change themselves. Unfortunately, in a very important respect, many communards emulate the system they condemn. As it was in the movement, so in most communes our brothers and sisters value above all the freedom to "do their own thing." And doing your own thing is nothing more than competing. Rather than trying to prove our worth by being the best kid in class or the rising young executive we try to prove it by being the most original mind, the best craftsperson, the natural leader, the most liberated woman, the most spiritually advanced. While we have dropped out of competing for money and the power this society has to give, most of us have not stopped trying to achieve the grand prize in the affections and approval sweepstakes. We still try to achieve a sense of belonging built on being better at something, anything. And for us to be better, a brother or sister has to be proven worse.

Without comparisons there would be no competition and, without both, there'd be no greed, envy, war. If we could make our communal societies work like the traditional Indian ones did, we'd be glad for the happiness and achievements of our brothers and sisters. We wouldn't try to top them. We'd know that we were all important parts of the universe and so we wouldn't compete to get feelings of belonging and being loved. We'd be free to truly love, to free others from their cages built of fear.

Emotional habits—especially negative ones—die hard. Being insecure, unhappy, complaining, competing is familiar emotional ground. Being secure, happy, and cooperative is not. Most of us would rather stick with the familiar, even if we hate it, just because we're afraid of the unknown. To make our own fledgling societies work we have to learn to effectively dispose of our own negativity. To do that we have to watch ourselves as we live our lives, seeing and accepting our actions without judgement or fear. Eventually we will see enough good that we'll begin to really like ourselves. As this liking grows, so does our confidence and security. When we find enough real love in ourselves for our own spirits we can begin to live with real balance and to create the kind of tribal society that will make us all free to be what we are—joyful creatures of the universe.

What you believe you become. Believe in beauty, for the Earth Mother is covered with beauty. Believe in love, for your Earth Mother and Sky Father love you. Believe in magic, and you release your soul from the prison your mind tries to build around it. Above all, don't be afraid. The Great Spirit provides all that is needed. Believe in your medicine. Believe in the work you are doing to become an instrument of the Great Spirit's will. Believe that you are where you should be. Believe that your life is progressing to its proper destiny. Believe in beauty, believe in love, believe in magic, and you will realize you are beautiful, loving, and magical.

Hey—hey yo hey—he yo—HO!

Grandfathers and Grandmothers
Great Spirit
We give thanks for this day
We give thanks for your Light.

The Light you have put within
   each of us grows brighter.
It shines through us, reaching out
   to Light our paths,
Illuminating for others their own
   spark of Light.

The People are
   bathed in this Light
Soon they will be complete
   once again.

As the Spirit grows,
   as your Light spreads,
The People will grow
   Oppression will end.

Greed will go, taking with it
All of its dark helpers:
   hatreds, envies, fears,
   violence, sicknesses, wars.

In your Light all darknesses
of the Soul disappear.

Eagles soon will soar across
  the land,
telling of your Light.
In their talons they hold—
  for all to see—
The mended hoop of the Nation.

Brothers, Sisters, two-leggeds,
four-leggeds, the people of the air,
those of the water, those who live
within the womb of the
  Earth Mother,
and grow upon her—

All will gather
  To celebrate Your Light.

All the differences, divisions,
  and fears
will disappear.

All will be truly One.

It is good.

HO!

—Wabun
for the Bear Tribe

II

Relating to the Earth Mother

The entire following section comes from Wabun's studies with Sun Bear and other Native medicine persons.

Coming into Harmony

We must learn to love our Earth Mother and the other beings who dwell with us on her with the emotional force we usually reserve for loving our dearest human friends. When you learn to do this you will transform yourself, and help the transformation of the earth. Some people are able, naturally, to love the earth in this manner. Others have to learn how to give themselves the space to do it. It is helpful to find an area that feels really good to you: one in which you feel safe, protected, and loved. Go to visit this area whenever your heart tells you to. Always thank the area for giving you such good feelings. Take the area presents of tobacco or corn-meal. Pray there. Sing there. Dance there. Feel yourself merging with this part of the Earth Mother. Feel her merging with you. Be patient. Don't resist your feelings. If it is meant to happen, one day you will feel your heart fill with that place. You will yearn to see it, as you once yearned to see a loved one's face. You will know that you've taken the first step in learning to really love Mother Earth, and the rest will come.

Praying

Too many of us have forgotten how to pray for anything outside of our own wants. We have forgotten that the Earth Mother and our fellow creatures also need our prayers. We have forgotten that praying for these others is one of our responsibilities as human beings. How often do you tell the trees they are beautiful? How often do you compliment the birds on the beauty of their song? How often do you thank the spirit of the water for the many gifts

39

she brings you? How often do you thank Earth Mother for sustaining your life?

Prayers don't need to be the complicated, eloquent prose offerings many of us have grown up with. All they need to be is sincere. If your heart speaks in eloquent language, fine. If your heart speaks as a child, that is beautiful, too. Pray often. Pray when you feel it. Be abundant with your thanks. Explain to other forces of nature what you need when you have need of them.

If you are planting something, go to the area beforehand, and tell those of the mineral kingdom what it is you wish to do. Ask them for their help and support. Ask them to feed the plant people you will be putting there. Thank them for being there. Thank them for all that they have to give. Thank them for working with you. Tell them of your need for them, and of your appreciation.

If you must disturb them, ask them to understand. If you must destroy some rocks, tell them why. Assure them that you, too, will someday be food for the Mother Earth.

It is the same when you deal with your brothers and sisters in the plant and animal kingdom. Always show them love and respect. Always treat them as equal partners in the work you are doing—whether it is planting a garden, harvesting, birthing a lamb, or butchering a cow. If your attitude is sincerely prayerful, loving, and respectful, your fellow beings will help you in whatever it is that you have to do.

Nature Spirits

If you show a good attitude to the beings who work with us on the physical plane, the beings from other planes will note what you are doing, and will try to help you. The spirits of the planet are very much present. They are willing to help, they are willing to reestablish their proper relationship with human beings. All they need is to know of your sincerity, of your respect.

Don't have expectations about what it will be like contacting nature spirits. Don't expect to see elves and leprechauns sitting on all of your plants. Different spirits take different forms. Many don't take form at all. Some humans are capable of seeing spirits; others, of hearing them; others, of sensing their presence. Have faith in your way of making contact. Believe in those things that you feel to be true. When you are sailing in uncharted territory—and dealing with spirits today is surely that—the heart is the most reliable navigator. Move gently among the spirits. Accept them. Understand them as best you can. And have patience. What seems impossible today may seem like the most natural thing in the world a month or a year from now.

Celebrations

One of the best ways to show our love for Mother Earth and the Great Spirit is through celebrations of their unity, and the unity of all creation. Our celebrations are based upon our knowledge of the traditional way, but they are not copies of old celebrations. We feel that this is a new time, and that our celebrations must reflect the time we are in and the heart feelings that we have. While we respect the old ways we know that feelings are more important than form. And that is how it was in the even older way that is remembered in the hearts of a few.

The Circle

We use the circle several times each day. When we pray in the mornings and evenings, we come together in a circle. Before eating, we join hands in a circle. Before sweating, we gather in a circle. When we council, we sit in a circle.

The circle reminds us that all life is continuous, that there is no beginning or end, that all flows together in perfect harmony.

We also have a medicine wheel on our land. At this circle we make our special prayers and give thanks for our connections with the universe and with the power that such special circles can bring.

The Pipe

We use the pipe at many times. When we are about to council, when we have another celebration, when we pray for healing,

when we pray with thanks we make smoke. We are blessed to have several pipes to use for medicine. We have our tribal pipe. We have the pipe of Yellow Hand, a Cheyenne chief killed by Buffalo Bill. This came to us from another medicine man. Sun Bear has his own pipe for special medicine, and we have another pipe used only for particular kinds of medicine. Many of our members also have their own pipes.

The pipe represents the universe. The bowl is made of stone from the mineral kingdom. The stem is made of wood from the plant kingdom. When we bring out the pipe, we acknowledge our relationship to these other kingdoms. The tobacco is the ritual victim which gives itself so that our prayers may rise to the Great Spirit. When we place the tobacco in the pipe we offer a pinch for each of these kingdoms, for the spirit world, for our fellow two-leggeds, for the powers of the four directions, and for any special healing or prayer we are making. After lighting the pipe we then offer smoke for each of the directions, for the Earth Mother, and for the Great Spirit.

Using the pipe helps us to remember our connection with all of the universe.

The Sweat

In the sweat lodge we are cleansed in our bodies, our minds, our hearts, and our spirits. Through the marriage of earth, fire, water, and air, this cleansing comes about. We enter in our ignorance and fear, and, through grandfather and grandmother's breath, we come out as new beings, better able to know the love of the Great Spirit and the compassion of the Earth Mother.

The sweat lodge is built from any young hardwood sapling. After proper prayers the trees are cut and then bent into a dome shape and lashed together. The lodge is covered with canvas or blankets or sleeping bags, or with mats woven from grasses, or with mud. The door of the lodge faces east. A fire pit is built outside. Rocks are obtained from a riverbed or volcanic area, as these rocks will not break when they are heated as granite ones will.

Before the sweat, the firekeeper puts the rocks in the fire pit, then builds a fire over them. When they are really hot, the sweat is ready to begin. The firekeeper takes a rock from the fire for each of the directions, for the Earth Mother, and Great Spirit. He or she carries them in a sun-wise direction around the fire pit, and then places them in a pit in the center of the lodge. Additional rocks may be put inside. The people enter the lodge in a sun-wise direction. Water is placed on the rocks and the sweat ceremony begins. If there is a leader, he or she makes prayers for each of the directions. They may also open the flap to invite in the power of the directions. They make prayers for Earth Mother and Great

Spirit. Songs may be offered. Others may offer their prayers. Water is passed around the circle. When the time feels right, we exit in the opposite direction from that in which we entered. We give thanks for the sweat, for feeling clean and good, and for the time we have been able to share together. The sweat is one of the most powerful Native ceremonies. It should only be conducted by people well trained in its form and spiritual substance.

Planting and Harvesting

We celebrate the time of planting by giving thanks to the Earth Mother for the season in which she brings forth in such abundance. The sisters offer cornmeal and make their prayers, and they then circle the fields that will be planted, asking that the power of creation that they have been given will join with the creative power of Earth Mother.

After our harvest, we give thanks for all the goodness that the Earth Mother and our plant brothers and sisters have given us. We pray that the time of rest for the earth and the spirits will be good and refreshing.

Earth Renewal

Our biggest celebration of the year comes at the time of the winter solstice, the time of earth renewal. At this time, when the sun is at its furthest point away from us, we have four days of fast. During these days we remember that without the warmth and light of Father Sun returning to heat the Earth Mother and make her grow, life would not continue. We fast and pray that Father Sun will return, that the cycle of life will continue. On the day that the sun begins its return, we take a sweat to cleanse ourselves of all the old so that we may greet the new year as new humans. On this day the sisters join together to grind the sacred cornmeal for the year in the old way, with a stone grinding bowl and pestle. This cornmeal is used during the year when we wish to make an offering for fertility and abundance. On Earth Renewal day we offer some cornmeal and ask that the year coming be a good one for the Earth Mother, and for all people. We then have a day of ceremony, feasting, and fun, and we invite our friends to come and join with us.

It is important to remember the life-giving sources of Creation, and the reality that we can't create them ourselves. The traditional Native didn't take the return of the sun for granted, but was thankful and joyful each time it happened. Because of the way most of us were educated, we are taught to expect the beginning of winter as a given, not as a gift. This has changed our attitude from one of thankfulness to one of expectation, allowing us to extract from Earth's resources without acknowledgment or return. The ceremonies of Earth Renewal are one of the ways we say, "Thank You."

There is a growing awareness of ceremony in the last decades. More and more workshops, seminars, and lectures are being given on its importance. More people are organizing groups that meet together for a variety of homemade and learned ceremonies, songs, and dances honoring Earth and her resources.

We celebrate the summer solstice, and the spring and autumn equinox by fasting, sweating, doing pipe ceremony, having a spirit feast, praying, and giving thanks for the turning of the wheel of life.

Singing, Drumming, Dancing

The whole universe dances to the song of creation. When we sing and dance we join in this union. When we drum, we hear the merging of the heartbeat of our body with that of the Earth Mother and of the drum. It is good to give thanks in these ways.

The Circles of Life

In the old days, each time of a person's life had a special texture, a certain taste, and each phase was honored, respected, and enjoyed. Life was seen as a flowing circle, from birth to death to rebirth. The circle of life, like the circle of the seasons, flowed smoothly but had division. After the dawn of birth and infancy, we all experience the spring of our youth, the summer of adulthood, the fall of middle age, and the winter of our older years.

In the old ways, the beginning of each phase of life, like the beginning of each season, was celebrated by the people. The celebration of each new stage in a person's life made the transition into this stage more definite and more pleasant. With the celebration came the knowledge that one stage of life, with its pleasures and responsibilities, had ended, and a new one had begun. While there might be regret at the passing of some favored pastimes, there would also be expectation of new tasks, lessons, and jobs to come.

At the time of birth, parents, elders, and relatives celebrated the gift of life given to the family and the tribe. They presented the child to the Creator, Father Sun, and Earth Mother, and they bestowed a name upon the new spirit now among them. By doing so they acknowledged that the child was a gift of life given to the Earth Mother by the Great Spirit, and that the child had a mission to fulfill, a prayer to pray, and a song to sing that was all his own.

When a child became a youth and was able to take on some of the responsibilities of the tribe's physical and spiritual survival, there was another celebration. Sometimes the youth was given another name that better reflected his or her true nature.

When a young man had his first successful hunt or when a young woman had her first moon, there were celebrations to honor them in the new phase of life they had entered. For a young woman, this celebration of her moon marked her entry into womanhood. Young men were not considered adults until they had successfully sought their vision. The celebration of this event was often a quiet and small one between the individual and the medicine people aiding them. While men had to seek vision to be complete, women, in most tribes, were also free to do so.

When people were adults, there were celebrations to mark important times that ushered them into new phases of life. There were celebrations for the joining of life paths—either through marriage, adoption, or the making of relatives. There were celebrations for births and for times of changing worlds. There were celebrations when one became an honored elder in the tribe.

These celebrations helped to give each circle of life its special texture and taste. Beyond that, these celebrations constantly reminded the people of their intimate and lifelong connection with the spiritual side of life. Another function of personal celebrations in the old ways was that they made people acknowledge changes in their lives and so prepare for the next lessons life had to bring them. They helped people to know that change meant growth, not loss.

Admittedly, this lesson is easier to learn in a society that lives close to nature. In such a society you need only look at the plants to know that seeds held too long by a plant rot rather than grow. It is the same with the cycles of humans. If we hold on to one stage of our lives too long, we crystallize rather than grow.

Celebrations of the changing fabric of our lives can help us to grow. They are needed as much now as they were in the old days.

Freeing the Sister
Within

Following is Wabun's personal account of beginning to learn to free the sister within her.

Until I was thirty, I always harbored a secret wish to be a man. I remember as a child I always envied the little boys. They seemed so much freer. Growing older, I learned well to emulate the men I saw around me. I became competitive, and I pushed to excel at any of the things I chose to do. I did not have a strong physical body, and so I developed my mind. I was an excellent student. I learned to manipulate, and I became a student leader. I went into politics, and knew how to be elected to any offices I wanted to hold, up to a point, that point being when I threatened the men I worked with too much. Then they put me down. After one such incident, I stopped being political. I turned to writing, which I had always been good at doing. I went to the best journalism school in the United States, and I did well. When I tried to get a job, after over $20,000 worth of education, I found that, as a woman, I only qualified as an assistant to a man. This was before women's lib, and jobs were not being equally doled out. I found a man I could enjoy working with, and helped start several new magazines. Finally, I was made editor of one. Still, all my decisions were censored by the men backing the magazine. I felt powerless.

I freelanced, writing about what interested me, mainly radical politics and the human-potential movement. I wrote a book which was published by a major New York publisher. By that time, I had realized that my satisfaction had to come from within, not without. I became involved in searching for a spiritual teacher, someone who could tell me how to become free. While involved with a Sufi-oriented group in New York, I met Sun Bear and decided I wanted to write about him and the Bear Tribe. Because of the love I felt for him and his work, I left New York and came to live with the Tribe. I became his medicine helper.

What a learning experience that was and is. Being in such close association with a strong man, I had to really fight to keep any sense of my own identity, my own worth. We both had to learn to work with each other without losing our separate balances. I felt that the struggle was worthwhile since he was a man who was not afraid of my energy and my strength. He encouraged me to develop all the skills I had, to develop my powers. Still, things did not feel quite right. There was a missing element.

Within the last years, I have found what that is. It is my femininity—my true essence of womanhood. I had always been a highly intuitive person, though, until recently, I could not have even found the words to express that. I just knew that often I thought differently from people around me, and that sometimes this got me into trouble. I'd know things that other people couldn't see, and I would know them from some source of knowing that I could not explain. I remember one man friend once listening to me expound on how I felt about things and then saying, "You're impossible. You have no comprehension of the basis of Western civilization." He was right, and I thank the Great Spirit for sparing me that.

The past years have been a time for many to realize that female energy must be allowed to develop and strengthen. I have been helped in my search to find my essence by others who are also seeking. Many beautiful sisters have helped me, by finding the beauty and ability to carry on, and by reflecting my own beauty and strength back to me. The Earth Mother has helped me, as I have finally been able to open myself to her. Spirits wishing to correct the imbalance between male and female energies have helped also. So has my deepening understanding of the Native people and how they related to the Earth.

To Native people, life is a circle of energy. Even after European people came here, the Natives acknowledged that energy in their names for the Creator, which were always verbs. In the limitations of the English language, the most common translation for the Chippewa word for the Creator would be "the Great Spirit" or "the Great Mystery." A more accurate translation, albeit one that is also limited, would be "the great and wondrous mystery that is around all things and within all things, that has no beginning nor ending but always is."

Native people respected that energy and the circle of life. They knew that anything you did to one part of the circle would eventually affect every other part. That means that if you limit humans, if you deny their natures, you will eventually deny the nature of the Earth herself. That is what civilizations in recent history have done.

To the Native people of old, women were the reflection of the Earth Mother, as men were the reflection of Father Sun. Some Natives have told me that the basis of their belief system even now is that "all things are born of woman," as all things are born of the Earth. But when women in more recent history were perceived as being dangerous to the civilization being built because of their childbearing capacities or their menstrual energies, so too was the Earth perceived as dangerous. As we were taught to fear the feminine, we learned to fear the Earth.

It does follow. The Earth, like a good mother, nurtures all of us from the moment of our birth onto the planet until the day of our death. She gives us the things we need for life: air, water, soil in which to grow food, beauty in abundance to feed the eyes and the soul, the sounds of the winds, the dance of the trees. In a similar way our human mothers also nurture us, giving us the milk of life, the touch of love, the safety in which we grow.

When the Earth was inhabited by cultures that revered the feminine, these cultures also saw the Earth as sacred. When the tides of history brought cultures that revered the masculine, all things female—including the Earth—became suspect. To build and maintain a culture in which men were primary, women had to become secondary. To construct a civilization in which competition overwhelmed cooperation, in which possessions counted more than people, in which taking what you need for the present became more important than preserving the Earth for all generations to come, people had to learn to view the planet as a lifeless backdrop for their pursuits.

The older Native cultures saw the Earth as a living being with her own vision to follow and destiny to pursue. As they respected all things feminine, they also respected the Earth. They knew they had to give back to her in order for the circle of life to continue in a healthy manner, and they knew the ways of making these gifts. Native people saw humans as receivers and transmitters of energy, much like the trees. They knew people could give their energy to the Earth and so help the Earth continue to prosper. Native people taught their children that they could give to the Earth by really looking at her beauty, thereby transmitting energy with their eyes. They could give to the Earth by listening to her songs and singing them back to her, by letting their feet dance in rhythm with the heartbeat of the planet, by keeping a prayer of thanksgiving in their hearts, by giving gifts of tobacco and cornmeal. At times, Native people would put all these energies together and have ceremonies of thanksgiving to the Mother of all. There are many stories I've heard about the consequences that occur when people forget to give back to the Earth and disturb the circle of life. We are seeing many of these consequences in the world today.

The view this society holds of the Earth is very different from the older Native ones. The Earth is most often seen as a mere backdrop for the important affairs of humans, as a source of unlimited resources that make people more comfortable. Since the early Europeans first set foot upon this continent they have seen the land as an "unspoiled wilderness" waiting to be plundered as they manifested their destiny from sea to sea. The Earth and her resources are seen as something to own and use and then discard with little regard for the effects the garbage might also bring to the Earth. Perhaps the worst lie of all in this society is that technology can correct any problem that it causes. Even with the devastation caused by acid rain and the depletion of the ozone layer, even with states fighting to keep nuclear dumps outside their territory, many people still believe we can live better through technology.

Some of us know better. Almost every Native culture I've encountered has some prophecies that speak of this time upon the planet as a time of changes in which the Earth will begin to rid herself of the poisons that humans have created. Although the details of these prophecies vary, they do have common threads. Most of them speak of the dangers of nuclear destruction, be it from bombs, waste, or ever-increasing levels of radiation. Many of them allude to the possibility of another large war, to ever-increasing seismic and volcanic activity, to changes in the planetary weather that will make it difficult to grow food, to drought, to famine, and to a large reduction in the human population. Many of these prophecies also say humans can have some effect upon the severity of the Earth cleansing.

An image that often comes to my mind is that contemporary humans are like the fleas on the back of a beautiful shaggy dog named Earth. If the fleas aren't too greedy, the dog lets them be. But when they start going deeper into her flesh, she tries to shake them off. If they get smart and stop biting, she stops shaking, but if they continue she shakes harder and harder and begins to scratch at the greediest and most annoying ones until, one way or another, she gets rid of them. So it is with us and the Earth now. We are sucking her life blood, and she occasionally shakes her body to warn us to stop. If we heed these warnings and stop taking from the Earth without regard for her needs or for the generations to come, the Earth will allow us to continue living upon her. If we ignore the warnings, the shakings will become more severe.

There are many things we can do right now to help the Earth. Begin by realizing the vast connection we have with her. Try to understand that in many real ways, the Earth is our Mother. Treat the Earth as you feel a good mother should be treated: with love, honor, and respect. Become sensitive to the Earth. Give her the gift of your energy. Consider praying or creating ceremonies to express your gratitude. Feel her energy within you. Allow yourself to be attuned to the changes her changing atmosphere has upon you, as people from the old Native cultures observed the Earth and the changes she made upon them.

We are living in times in which we have to make personal changes that allow us to come to know, nurture, and free the more natural person living within each one of us. That means, among others things, that we must face our own fears about the "dark" and the sexual sides of our beings. At the same time we need to do everything we can to help the planet and the other beings who dwell with us upon her before the ecological disasters overwhelm all of life. Understanding is the key. The more we understand ourselves, the more we understand every other part of the circle of life. But understanding, even wisdom, isn't enough. We must act upon what we know if we wish to preserve life, not just for this generation, but all for generations to come. Our understanding and actions must be guided by as much honesty as we are capable of facing about ourselves and our relationship to the Earth.

You can't say that you love the earth and act in a disrespectful way to women, or to the female energy inside of you. If you don't love the human representation of the energy of the earth, you don't really love the earth. When I look at the period of cleansing on the earth now, I know that part of the reason for the cleansing is the things that we have done externally—poisoning the water, poisoning the air, poisoning the earth. Another part comes from the fact that we have poisoned ourselves, internally, by fearing the female energy within. I can't separate these two and say if we take care of ecology, everything on the earth is going to be fine, because I know, within myself, that that is not true.

We can't cleanse the earth without cleansing the female energy in each one of us. We can't get back to a place of love and respect and responsibility for the earth until we come to a place where we love and respect the female energy that we all have. It takes a lot of work for us who are in female bodies, and even more for brothers, because their conditioning has been different.

We must begin to trust our own perceptions and intuitions and use the wisdom they give us in our everyday lives. Native people were so aware of the necessity of everyone using their intuition that tribal men were required to go seek their vision. Without the vision, they were considered to be incomplete. Those of us who have gone out for a vision know that the vision comes from the perceptions, from receptivity, from the female part of the being. By seeking a vision a man had to open to his female energy, and this did help him to be complete.

Native life, with its times of physical endurance and the necessity for strength, forced women to use their physical beings in such a way that they had to learn about their male energy. They learned to discriminate, to be strong and enduring. They, too, learned to become complete by opening to both the energies within them.

We all carry within us some fear of the raw, emotional energy that we sometimes feel. Maybe you feel it more during full moon, or, if you are a sister, during your own moon time. We fear this energy because it confounds the rational mind and because it is so intense. We're afraid to let it come out, so we push it deeper down, and it gets darker and more frightening the deeper we push it.

Now we're in a period of time when we have to learn to channel this energy. First, we have to recognize that it exists. Then we must become familiar with it. To do so, we must find people we can trust enough to begin to open some aspects of ourselves that we've always kept hidden. We must be patient and gentle with ourselves during this process. People who let too much of their hidden aspects come out at one time often become afraid and retreat even deeper into their shells. We must begin to understand our own female energy, and how it relates to the earth, and the moon, and the waters.

It's a really delicate balance that all of us have to learn right now. We must learn how to be responsible to the earth and, at the same time, how to open ourselves to the real female and male energies within. We must balance these with all of the other work of service that needs to be done on the earth at this time. Sensitive people may feel like they are walking a very slender tightrope. But all of us on that rope have chosen to be here now because the chance for personal, as well as earthly, evolution is so great.

I know that those of us who can open now must do so, so that we can be there to help others through the challenge of freeing the sisters within themselves. I have a glimmering of the joy that will eventually come through this freeing.

III

Communities

This section is drawn from Sun Bear, Nimimosha, and Wabun's experiences with the Bear Tribe, other communities, and medicine societies.

Rebirth of Medicine Societies

Many people today are looking for ways to restore the spiritual values and traditional ways of people. They know that Native Americans were a people who had a strong reverence for and belief in the Great Spirit.

As they look around in these times and see the continuous deterioration of this system, they are looking for stronger values. They see that the way the white man's Sunday religion works is that people go to church on Sunday and then they steal and cheat each other all the rest of the week. They see a nation that claims to be Christian and yet plunders Native lands and continues to hold back justice from many people.

Native prophecies predicted this time thousands of years ago. The time will come, the ancient teachings say, when the sons and daughters of our oppressors will return to us and say, "Teach us so that we might survive; for we have almost ruined the earth now." Many modern people are now examining the values of the old ones, the values that were life-affirming. These people search the old ways, asking themselves, "What were the ideals of old that kept Natives strong and true in their hearts?"

One answer is that medicine people and medicine societies were the center of a tribe. Before the crop was planted, proper prayers and medicine for success were made, prayers and ceremonies of thanksgiving were done. In every major undertaking of the tribe, the medicine was first consulted. The consideration was always, is this act in harmony with Creation? Is it in harmony with life? Is it in harmony with the sacred journey we are on?

To get back to the old values, people must learn to live together in strong tribal groups that are interdependent with one another. It is not simply a matter of copying the outward forms practiced centuries ago. It is not a matter of rejecting technological developments or social structures. To reestablish decent values people need to learn love and harmony for one another and for the earth. They must listen to their own medicine, to the voice within, the voice which is in harmony with life. They must learn all they can, and then let go of it all, to learn *new* ways of relating to our Earth Mother, new ways of relating to one another, new ways of responding to the changing needs of the earth. They have to learn that they can't lean on the past, but must allow the Earth Mother and the race called humanity to continue their paths of destiny. They must release themselves from the idea that all will be as it once was. Life continues to move forward. In these conditions, medicine societies will become alive again and they will allow the peaceful, gentle forces to work at establishing true harmony on our Earth Mother.

History of the
Bear Tribe

People who are drawn to medicine societies and communities are often motivated by wanting to be part of something larger than themselves. In coming to such an alternative, they find they have chosen a way that will sometimes be painful, sometimes challenging, sometimes exhilarating, and always growth-producing. They can no longer hide from their old attitudes, wounds, limitations, and fears. They can no longer pursue "personal freedom" as though nobody else existed. In community, they must learn the meaning of responsibility to themselves, to Spirit, to the earth, and to the others with whom they share their lives. The following is Wabun's account of her experience in being with the Tribe during her first four years of community, with some updates as to the Tribe's structure now.

The Bear Tribe is This One's vehicle for learning how to work, and how to believe. The Bear Tribe is a modern day medicine society composed of Indian and non-Indian people. We have been brought together by the medicine and the vision of Sun Bear, a medicine man of Chippewa heritage, and by our own visions. Sun Bear believes, because of his visions and dreams, that people must learn again how to be in harmony with each other and the Earth Mother.

The Bear Tribe consists of the people who live and work together on Vision Mountain or at our Circle Center in Spokane, and of the apprentices who work with us from their homes all around the world. We have been together for varying lengths of time. During these years many other people have come to the Tribe and left, either at our request, or because they felt we asked too much of them, or because their path was elsewhere. We have few laws that people pledge themselves to when they take their oath to the

Tribe. We make a promise to try to build a relationship of true love and responsibility to our brothers and sisters, and to abstain from the use of drugs. We also commit ourselves to a goal of non-possessiveness and gentleness. We give a portion of our resources to the Tribe, and in return, the Tribe assumes responsibility for many of our needs: physical, mental, emotional, and spiritual.

Our aim is to be in harmony with ourselves, with each other, with the Earth Mother, and with the will of the Great Spirit.

To accomplish our aims we must first learn to be in harmony with ourselves and each other. To do this, we live and work together. Learning to live and work with a group of people is not as easy as it may sound. All of us now in the Tribe came to it tainted by the dominant society which teaches competitiveness and possessiveness. It teaches us that we must be number one, no matter what the cost to those who are around us, to those we profess to love. It teaches us that our "personal freedom" is paramount. It teaches us that love, trust, and responsibility are commodities to be sold to the highest bidder. It teaches us to be insecure, fearful, and cynical. It teaches us that the law is there to oppress people who are inherently bad.

To live in harmony with ourselves and with a group of people, we must constantly work to unlearn all of the things the dominant society has taught us. We must work to learn to cooperate instead of compete, to share instead of possess. We must learn that we are one unique and important part of the whole, but not the only one. We learn to surrender "personal freedom"—doing our own thing—when our own thing will be destructive to the Society. We must learn that love, trust, and responsibility are real feelings that grow with time, with work shared, and respect earned. We work to learn to be secure from within, knowing that we are a part of the Earth Mother, and of a Medicine we all respect and cherish. We learn to trust our medicine, so we have no need of fear. We learn to always look at the wonders of the Earth Mother and each other with fresh and open eyes, so there is no room for cynicism.

We learn to see our laws as something we must measure up to in our own hearts, not as things that oppress us. We strive to see that to build a true medicine society, our words and actions must always be measured by how they will affect the Earth Mother, the Great Spirit's will, the Society, and our brothers and sisters. We learn to listen to the council of our brothers and sisters, and to the consensus of our council circle. We learn to trust that our circle, and the others in it, can sometimes see truths about ourselves that we don't want to see.

To put all of this into practice in our daily lives with each other we must learn to be happy, no matter what we are doing. We must learn to see that all work—seeking medicine, doing dishes, digging cesspools, building houses, writing articles, answering letters, drawing pictures, doing craft work, teaching children, growing gardens—is a way of developing ourselves, and our strength as a circle. We must learn that different people have different gifts, and different levels of energy, and that we are not being "exploited" if, at some times, we are doing more outward work than the others in the circle. We must learn to share our gifts, rather than hoarding them, and to be happy if some other one excels at something we previously had done "best." We must learn to take responsibility, and then to give it away when another is ready to have it. We must learn to be proud of our accomplishments, yet humble in knowing that everything that allows us to accomplish is a gift from the Great Spirit.

To live in harmony we must practice the age-old virtues of charity, humility, love, patience, and compassion for others and ourselves. This is a big order to fill, considering the backgrounds most of us come from. Twentieth-century survival and "success" do little to support such virtues as compassion, or letting go of anything without first acquiring a replacement for it.

One key to letting go is trust, most often, trust that a decision to let go will bring about higher good. The caution we need to exercise here is not to confuse "higher good" with personal wishes, or with our preconceived notions of the outcome. If this confusion exists, the act of "letting go" can become a manipulation—just the opposite of letting go. Most of us still fear the sense of loss we expect to feel if we let go of something or someone. How will we refill the void left within us? Will we become unimportant and unfulfilled? The things we have to let go of are difficult—fear, hiding in our "privacy," being a particular kind of person, old habits and attitudes, and our expectation that we can make these changes quickly and completely simply by wanting to. This process requires compassion, a skill we each have to learn for ourselves, as well as for others.

While striving to be in harmony with each other, we must also learn to be in harmony with our common Earth Mother and all of her other children. This too, takes work, practice, and patience. The society that we have come from teaches that nature is a fearful thing, something to be harnessed and controlled by man. It also teaches that mankind is supreme, and has rightful dominion over the four-leggeds, the people of the air, and the people of the water.

Consequently most of us have some fear of the Earth Mother and her creatures. It takes time to become at ease with the sounds of the country as we are with those of the city. It takes work to realize that the climatic changes on the earth are necessary for her development, and not something to curse when they foil our plans. We must learn to enjoy the sounds of the many winds, the roar of the thunder beings, the clash of lightning bolts. We must learn to see a snowstorm as a thing of beauty, not an inconvenience. We must learn to fall on ice, and slide in mud, and trust the Earth Mother to catch us.

Especially in this time of earth changes we must trust that the sudden floods, the unexpected tornadoes, the droughts, the earthquakes are all necessary happenings that will return the Earth Mother to a state in which she can bloom again, cleansed of the poisons with which man has polluted her.

We strive to learn love and respect for our little brothers and sisters who fly in the air, swim in the water, walk on four legs, and grow on the earth. We learn, through observation, that they, too, have a place on our Mother, and functions they must perform for her. We learn that no creature is a pest, although some are destined to bring pestilence to those two-leggeds who have no respect for our Mother. We learn from these little ones, for often they have knowledge or instincts that we lack. We can learn what berries are good to eat and which are poisonous by watching whether our little brothers eat them. We can be forewarned of floods, storms, even earthquakes if we have learned to be in harmony with the little brothers and sisters.

We learn that killing for anything other than necessity is wrong. We always pray and offer smoke before taking the life of our little brothers. In our prayer, we tell our brother that we need his flesh to feed our own, that we realize our flesh, too, will become food for the Mother and her creatures, and we pray for his spirit to quickly go to our common Father. We always try to use every part of the animal we have killed.

We learn to extend the same respect to those in the plant kingdom. We never pick the wild plants without leaving an offering of kinnikinick, and telling them why we need them, and how they will help us. We never pick all of the plants growing in one area, for we realize that they must continue to grow and perform the work for which they were designed.

We learn to always offer prayers and, sometimes, ceremonies, before using a part of the Mother to grow those plants we need to eat. We offer the seeds to the Earth Mother, and ask her blessing so they may be fruitful. We also offer prayers to the seeds, asking them to grow, and telling them of our need for them. When we harvest any of our brothers in the plant kingdom we offer prayers of thanksgiving to them, and to the Earth Mother who has helped them to grow.

By learning respect for, and harmony with ourselves, each other, and the Earth Mother, we prepare ourselves to become instruments of the Great Spirit's will; to become medicine people of and for this time. Many times, Sun Bear has told us that the mistake most people make when they want to learn medicine is that they just want to go right to the mountain, before they have learned to walk with any balance on the Earth Mother.

"What would the Great Spirit want with a bunch of ding-a-lings who want to shake the rattle, but who don't even know how to be together without bashing each other's heads in, and scattering beer cans all over the Earth Mother?" he asks.

In the years that our group has been together we have learned through work, suffering, and struggles to be in better harmony with ourselves and with each other. It is often a pleasure now to sit in our council circle. We are constantly learning to love, to respect,

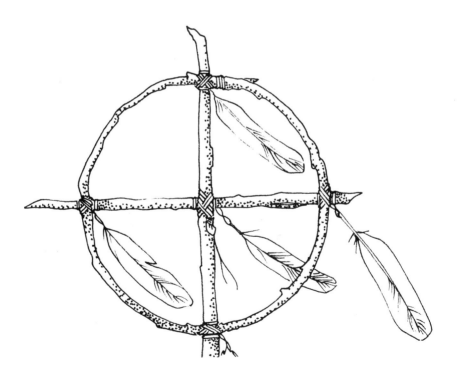

and to trust each other. On even the most difficult problems facing us we no longer need to struggle so much with each other. The medicine flows smoothly.

We have all come a lot closer to being in harmony with the Earth Mother, though we still have work to do in that direction. As long as we get mosquito bites, and have to scratch them, we are not in perfect harmony. But this, too, may come in time.

Daily, we are preparing ourselves to be instruments of the Great Spirit's will. We pray a lot, separately, and in a group, and our prayers, most often, are ones of thanksgiving. We have much to be thankful for. Often now, we sing together, and some of us dance old dances that have been given to us. Daily, we feel the medicine growing stronger in the circle, and in each of us who compose the circle. Each day we grow more receptive to the will of the Great Spirit, and to the voices of his helpers in the spirit world.

Before we were able to come to our degree of harmony, we as individuals, and the Tribe as an entity, had to experience difficult times. The Tribe began in California in 1970 when Sun Bear took the message of his vision to several universities and colleges in the Sacramento area. The response was so great that he soon had two hundred people living in seventeen base camps that had been given to the Tribe to use. In the summer of 1971, Sun Bear's medicine directed him to carry his message across the land. He did, with good results.

Upon his return to California he found that some camps were now using psychedelics. Since people joining the Tribe vowed to abstain from drugs, he felt sad. He went to a mountaintop to seek an answer.

As Sun Bear tells the story in *The Path of Power*, ". . . I saw a golden eagle. It circled around me while I lay there on the hilltop.

"I made my prayers, and I asked for a sign, for a direction. The eagle came and went, and he looked into my soul; I almost wept. I was joyful to have a sign from the Great Spirit, but I didn't know what it really meant.

"I stayed there; I prayed harder and harder. Suddenly, a huge white cloud came over me; it was the only cloud in a sky of perfect blue. As I prayed, the cloud came closer and closer; then a small puff of it separated off from the rest. A whirlwind came, and spun the little puff of cloud away. Part of it dissolved, but a fluff of it joined back with the large cloud. I knew, then, what would happen with the Bear Tribe, and I felt better.

"The Great Spirit had given me a sign; the people who were with me were not quite ready to live by my vision. Some would go back to the cities. Some would grow, and eventually find their

Yarrow, the first child born
into the Tribe, with Nimimosha

balance. And some, the vision told me, would only split off from
the Bear Tribe for a while; they were the little puff of cloud, and
they would return. The large cloud, the Bear Tribe itself, would
then blossom once again. I felt this in my heart."

Sun Bear then told people that he was leaving, as he could not
compromise his medicine. He invited those who wanted to follow
his medicine to come with him. Some did. Others stayed, mouth-
ing his ideals and hoping he'd change his mind. Eventually these
camps broke apart.

Over the next few years, Sun Bear, Nimimosha, some others,
and I worked to build a solid foundation for the Tribe. We moved
back onto the land, this time in Oregon. In 1975, because of the
direction of the medicine, we moved to Washington.

The Tribe now has sixty acres outside of Spokane. We have
large houses, cabins, root cellars, tipis, storage sheds, and animals.

We also have the Circle Center in town, where some of the
outreach activities of the Tribe are administered. Many of our
business functions take place there, including our bookstore, the
planning for Medicine Wheel Gatherings (which we put on three
or four times a year, drawing up to one thousand people to each),
for speaking and the apprentice program, for our magazine
Wildfire, for Bear Tribe Publishing, for fund raising, and for self-
help projects.

Sun Bear has apprentices around the world who actively work with us. Some of them have land bases, and others are moving in that direction. These apprentices form the core of our Medicine Wheel Network. They work in their own home areas to teach people about healing themselves and the earth.

Some Things
We've Learned

In the following section, Nimimosha, another medicine helper to Sun Bear, distills her more than twenty years of community living into helpful suggestions for anyone who has ever dreamed of forming or joining a community.

A community is a spiritual entity. It is a being with a birth, life, death, reason, emotion, perception, and the ability to grow and reproduce. It exists as such because the spiritual energy of individuals is channeled into it, merging with the energy of the spirits guiding it, creating its life force.

Love is the force that holds things together. Among people, it gives birth to families, communities, and nations. Without love, the harmonious energy of mutual enrichment is replaced with a perverted, chaotic energy of divisiveness. We can see this process happening all around us.

Perhaps it is necessary to explain what is meant by "love," since we seem to have lost this understanding. It is not sex, although physical touching may be involved. It is not romance or sentimental attachment. It is the force of Nature, by which all things can live together in harmonious abundance. It is the force of Creation, through which we gain our existence. It is the energy of positive mutual interest, which comes from the sharing of purpose.

For a community to survive, it is important to maintain a loving relationship among its members. We must always remember that we're here together for our mutual benefit. If we allow possessiveness or negativity to be expressed in our interpersonal relationships, or in our work, we create an energy field which weakens us. Neither should we deny our negative feelings, as they will then tend to come out in subtle ways. In cooperation and positivity we create a healthy atmosphere in which we can bring out and get rid of these divisive traits. This is a function of a healthy community.

Because we live closely in our community/medicine society, we have had to create healthy ways to prevent conflict, and to resolve conflict when it occurs. We agree that we do not wish to live with conflict as a daily reality with people we love, and so we ask a great deal of ourselves and each other. We ask each person to set aside his/her own sense of safety, and, using both honesty and compassion, resolve the conflict as soon as possible. We do not want our personal energies tied up in frustration, resentment, confusion, or anything negative. By resolving these feelings, our energy is then free to use for the life-affirming purposes for which we're together.

During the day we make medicine to strengthen our love as a community. Before each meal we join hands and give thanks for our nourishment and for our sharing as brothers and sisters. In the evening we sometimes form a circle to make prayers and reassert our togetherness. We share the pipe and sweat ceremony each week, and join together to celebrate the full moon, the equinoxes, and solstices.

It is also important to maintain a loving relationship with nature and our fellow beings. The trees, rocks, animals, sky, soil, and other beings need to share their love with us, and we need to love them. When we refuse, they are sad. The balanced energy flow is upset. Divisiveness replaces harmony, and the Earth Mother becomes ill. An example of this divisiveness is found in the concepts of property ownership and trespassing. Because property ownership is seen as a right, many property owners also assume the "right" to both abuse "their" land and keep other people away. This kind of possessive ownership is not in harmony, or in loving relationship with people or nature, and the result is most often disfiguring to the earth, and dispiriting to other beings. If we break our bond with the earth, the land and all beings on it can become ill. When the uniting energy of love is maintained, we can all share in nature's abundance.

Love of the Spirit is necessary to continue our mutually beneficial relationship with those spiritual beings who give us help. During our ceremonies we call together the spirits of the four winds, the plant, animal, and mineral kingdoms, asking for their guidance and help. We do this in a loving atmosphere, with an attitude of respect. By losing this reverent attitude for the spiritual beings, for the Spirit itself, modern people have forfeited this beneficial relationship. They are divided without and within. Relinquish the Spirit, relinquish your heart, and the mind and body fight for control. Love of the Spirit gives us internal strength, guiding us in the quest to achieve higher spiritual awareness.

Common Vision

Members must be in agreement on the purpose of a community, its goals, methods, and priorities. This common vision is necessary so that our energy is not dispersed in conflicting directions, but channeled toward a specific goal. The democratic system fails on this point. Forty-nine percent of the people can be in disagreement, thus undermining the effectiveness of the group. There should be a forum whereby each person has the chance to express his or her feelings and ideas.

For us, this forum is our Council Circle. It is our way of governing ourselves and for dealing with issues and decisions that must be made. When we have an issue that needs clarification or a decision that affects us all, or any matter we need to discuss, we have Council. We usually meet once a week, but, if our need changes, we may have more or fewer meetings of Council. In this Council, we bring our best selves, and observe a tacit agreement to listen well as each person speaks, not interrupting for any reason. In the early days, we often used a talking stick that the speaker held in his or her hand as a reminder to stay on subject, to speak the truth, to avoid filibustering, and to remind others that it is time for them to listen. We no longer need to use the talking stick. We have developed the ability to employ these skills without the stick.

In Council, everyone is given the opportunity to speak, though we discourage ourselves from becoming windbags. Everyone participates by making a contribution in the decision-making process. We no longer need it to be a lengthy process. We talk until we reach consensus. We remember that it is the medicine that guides us, not our individual thoughts or desires.

Being able to receive the guidance of the Medicine takes a great amount of trust, especially when we are first learning. Trust is the first quality one must attain in living the life of the Spirit, the first steppingstone on the Pathway of Peace. We must come to the realization that we always get what we need. If we are not experiencing joyful success, we are being sent a lesson. This happens by way of the balancing of natural forces. The energy which we put out is balanced by that which we receive. Nobody gets ahead of the game. There is no free lunch. Once we have this understanding, we can begin to see what the lessons are, and accept our guidance.

Sometimes it is difficult to hold onto our trust. In painful times we fall in despair, striking out at whatever or whoever is closest to us. When we begin to come back up, trust is right there, the first thing we have to learn and accept.

Today, many people still have faith in the medicine of the modern world, but many are beginning to lose it. That world no longer provides for the needs of its subjects, nor guides them in a positive manner. It is important to realize that when we lose our trust in that society we don't have to lose the ability to have trust in anything. The true medicine is waiting to help us whenever we seek it.

Keeping Order

One thing we can observe quite obviously when watching the workings of Nature is that she is orderly. Everything has a place and a purpose. There is no waste, nothing is ever lost. By maintaining this order, the greater whole, the Earth Mother, can function in a healthy manner, providing for the needs of all of her subjects. If the order is broken the balance is upset, and the needs are no longer met.

This principle can be practically applied within the community. The land, animals, buildings, equipment, tools, etc. have been placed here under our care and for our benefit. Fire hazards should be removed, animals should be fed and watered regularly, buildings maintained, work areas kept neat and convenient, tools put away.

The energy invested in establishing and keeping order is well worthwhile, as it makes for happier people and more efficient work of better quality. When we make a chair, cook a meal, or write an article, we are creating order from disorder. This can be more easily done in an organized environment, as it takes more energy to overcome the vibrations of chaotic surroundings. For brothers and sisters to live together harmoniously we should have a well-kept home. This makes for happier people in a stronger community.

Things should also be kept in order out of respect for the spirits of the things themselves. The kitchen should be bright and happy, not cluttered with messes and gloom. No self-respecting hammer wants to lie outside in the rain. If we truly care for it, we will place it in its proper resting place with a word of thanks. The spirit of the water hole doesn't mind our getting in to cool off if we act with respect, but she certainly doesn't want all that poisonous soap in her home. One should walk carefully among chickens, thanking them for their eggs and their energy.

Respect for one another is one of our greatest needs when

living close together. When someone fails to pick up after themselves or do their share of the chores, it's a drain on someone else. Someone who is sloppy in appearance and actions detracts from the good feelings of others. Balance must be maintained among those who don't care about neatness and those who do most of the cleaning up.

Many communities respond to this situation by setting up schedules and delegating responsibility, but we find that this interferes with the working of the Medicine. Each person must learn to see what needs to be done to balance out the load. Each person must participate by choice. It is Sun Bear's belief that the least governed are the best governed. This is an ideal we have all had to learn. This ideal will not be learned through criticism or scheduling, but through positive support, and through learning to see the larger picture of our relationship with each other. We have agreed on a high standard of neatness and quality workmanship, and we keep drawing our attention to this agreement. Learning to live with this agreement is a process, not an event. With plenty of tolerance, patience, and positivity, we are learning to achieve what we want.

When we move into a communal living situation we become painfully aware of our various problems left over from living in the modern world. These problems keep us from living harmoniously, and block our higher levels of awareness. There are many different theories about how to deal with these problems and better live together, and so there are many doctrines concerning organization, communication, cooperation, health, etc. Different communities are based on different theories, which serve to focus attention on a certain area of our improvement. Eventually, though, too rigid systems of thought will block individual expression and community growth.

We have frequently seen and felt the contradiction present in so many people, that while "lost" without an authority above us, or a visible chain of command, we feel the impulse to rebel against any form of hierarchy. Because of the culture and society that has formed us, we seldom know how to appropriately relate to authority, either in responding to it, or in taking it ourselves.

It has taken the exercise of patience to answer new visitors who first complain about our "disorganization," then complain when we do display organization. They wanted to know how they could fit in, but they didn't really want to be told. Had they been able to take note of the real authority—the order of Creation—they may have seen the need to be clean, to wash the dishes, and sweep the floor, before seeking the special experiences that come when a person is ready. As Sun Bear puts it, "How are you going to go to the mountain to meet the Creator if you can't get your dishes washed?"

We find it important to get along with a minimum of rules. People who are unwilling to do their fair share of the ordinary work cannot be allowed to stay. Daily chores, like washing dishes and maintenance, should be shared in some way that is equal, and it is each one's responsibility to make sure he or she does his or her own share. Some of us here have grown to have particular skills and knowledge for which the Tribe has great need—skills such as writing, typesetting, computer programming, administration—and are called upon at times to put most of their energy into these areas. These same people make sure that they do take part in the daily sharing of work whenever they can, so they don't forget the basics of their own home/community. For the most part, they have given most generously of their energies at the daily level.

We agree on priorities, and people are encouraged to do whatever is most important to them, or whatever is most in harmony with who they are. From time to time, we all must do something we don't enjoy because there is a need for it, but we try to allow each person to do the work they enjoy most, where positive spirit and pleasure in work can produce a positive and supportive environment.

Discipline

One quality we must have if we are to accomplish our goals, both personally and communally, is discipline. This may sound bad at first, because "discipline" has negative connotations. Discipline often has been forced upon us and has been unfair or irrational. In our reaction to this, many of us shun all concepts of discipline.

Discipline is the ability to set certain limitations and stick to them. It can be used to overcome forces which may attempt to sidetrack us from our chosen path. When we have a goal, we plan ahead how to work toward materializing it. While carrying out the plan we may meet up with new desires or ideas which make us think that some other activity is better. Discipline enables us to resist being sidetracked, and keep on with our work.

When some members of a group lack self-discipline, hence responsibility, it is important for others to assert enough leadership to keep the group on track. They supply the discipline for the group, to insure that projects are finished, standards met, guidelines adhered to, and lessons learned.

Responsibility

What we are striving for is to get free of planned existence, of leader-follower relationships. To do this, we must learn to take responsibility. Individuals must become clear-minded enough to be able to see what needs to be done, and to act on it in a positive way. We are each responsible for our own survival and well-being. If an individual cannot handle responsibility, he or she makes it necessary for someone or something else to lead them. The more we need to be led, the less we can hear the voices of our guidance or reach the higher levels of our creative expression. Without responsibility, one cannot attain medicine power.

At the same time, we need to turn loose our desires and expectations of others. If we try to assert our will too much over others, or over occurrences, the medicine cannot work. Other people cannot learn to hear the inner voices, and our own lessons cannot be received. We should be able to put our full attention into every task without worrying if something else is being done the right way (or our way). Then we can feel the approval of the Great Spirit in each of our accomplishments. The result of assuming responsibility and dropping expectations is freedom—not having to be led, nor to lead others. When we have achieved this, we will have achieved self-reliance, and we will be able to live together in harmony.

Patience

It is important to remember that it takes time to change. This is especially true for people who are coming to an alternative way of being. They need to adjust not only to new ways of thinking, acting, and perceiving, but to a whole different speed. It is important for all involved to give the process time to work. Putting oneself or others down for their shortcomings is one of the biggest things blocking improvement. This is part of learning compassion for ourselves and others. A good healer would avoid adding trauma to a wound. In the same way, demanding rapid change from a person often makes them cling more tightly to their old ways of being. In such situations, patience allows time for healing and for change.

By placing ourselves in a healthier environment, we ask to be guided toward health. We receive cleansing and lessons when we need them. If we try to force the changes before we're ready we upset the balance, creating negativity which must itself be overcome. Make sure that the change is in a positive direction, ask for help when it is needed, and wait for the process to work. Be guided not by concepts, but by the Spirit.

While you're waiting for yourself and others to change, develop your sense of humor. Laughter is always good medicine.

Be gentle to yourself and others. Remember how gentle the Earth Mother is to all of us.

Other Folks

This chapter is a note of honor from us to others who are striving to serve the Great Spirit, and our Earth Mother. We have heard about a lot of folks who are doing this, and we are honored to know some of them personally. We pray for all those we know, and those we've yet to encounter. It is so important to support the efforts of others on the same path on all of the levels that we can. Even if others walk with a different step, we support them for being on the good path.

The Rainbow Clan

Two friends who taught us a special way to pray and to spread the light are Joyce Rainbow and Richard Rainbow. He passed into the spirit world in 1985. They made their living selling turquoise and silver jewelry made by their clan.

"The whole clan believes in the old, traditional way," said Richard. "We are brothers to all living things. Everything is as important as we are, and we are as important as everything. We feel that the Grandfather Spirit guides our hands as we work so that we put the right stone with the right piece of silver to bring the maximum good or healing to the person who wears one of our pieces of jewelry."

The oldest members of the clan, Richard and his brother, Ted Bear, Sr., were both raised on the Miwuk tribal allotment in Tuolumne City, California. One hundred of the tribe's eighteen hundred members now live on this three-hundred-acre allotment. Their mother, almost a full-blood, was a member of the first tribal council back in 1935. Their father was Greek.

"When we were growing up on the reservation we were considered the Greeks. When we went into town we were considered the Indians. It was good because it was a growing situation. While we were growing up we were tutored by an old Miwuk medicine man who taught about herbs and about mentally making medicine. Our silverwork, too, started when we were kids. We used to tap coins into conchos or rings and then give the stuff away or sell it for a quarter."

Rainbow went to the Sherman Indian Institute in Riverside, then into the Navy, then to work for the Greek side of the family, where he remained for ten years learning about business and the white world. He went into business for himself, and continued until he got sick for eight months and lost everything. He made application for reinstatement as a tribal member, asked for an assignment, and was given fifteen acres. When he, Joyce, and their four children went to the reservation, Ted Bear, Sr., led him back into silversmithing. He also taught the craft to his own wife, Ramona, to their children and grandchild. The clan all works together now in a shop they own, the Tepee, located in the Tuolumne City Plaza.

When Rainbow returned to the reservation, he also began to work for an Office of Economic Opportunity–funded alcoholism program there.

"It wasn't hard for me to relate to the problems," Richard said. "I'd been a heavy drinker for thirty years before I quit that. But when I'd been doing alcoholism counseling for about six months, I got frustrated with the structured program. I was going to quit because I felt that I was doing no good. I worked with a hundred people, and had one success. I started looking for the common denominator of why Indian people drank. The thing that stuck out was that Indian people lacked spiritual expression. Where this did occur, like where people were heavy into Christianity, the alcoholism rate was low. I wrote a proposal for a program that would give Indian people the expression they lacked, and it was funded. I started talking to different medicine men. The first one I met was Ray Stone, a Paiute who conducts sweats. He came to the reservation three times, and he set up a sweat lodge on my assignment. Then David Villasenor, who does sandpainting, came to demonstrate that. At the 1973 Acorn Festival they both came. Ray ran the sweat for four days, and better than three hundred people were involved. David gave two sandpainting sessions, and six hundred people were there. And, for the first time, there was no drunkenness at the Festival, which would seem to show that the program is on the right track."

During his work with this program, the name Rainbow was given to Richard by a medicine man who told him his medicine comes from the Rainbow. He sees a real connection between his medicine work and his clan's work on silversmithing.

"To make our jewelry authentic, we've mixed our medicine

work with our silversmithing. When we work we ask that our hands be guided to make jewelry that will bring the wearer the happiness and harmony they seek, and we ask that every piece of jewelry will go to the right person.''

As Richard and Joyce traveled around the country to shows, they looked for people their medicine told them were ready to open to what they had to teach, and they taught them what they were capable of learning. Basically, they taught people their special way of praying and connecting themselves to the universe. They used the image of the rainbow and the light in their prayers. They sometimes invited people to their home, to sweat with them. Joyce Rainbow continues with the work she and Richard began.

Wolf Clan Lodge

Another friend who has generously shared her medicine with us is Twylah Hurd Nitsch, Clan Mother of the Wolf Clan Lodge. Yeh-weh-node, her Seneca name, means "echo" or "the voice that rides on the wind."

Twylah is both a powerful and peaceful woman. She grew up steeped in the wisdom of the Seneca way. Moses Shongo, one of the great Seneca medicine people, was her grandfather. Before her birth, he had worried about who was to take over the teachings. When Twylah was born he had said that since she had both Native and white blood, she would be able to walk on two paths, to move from the Indian to the white. When she was two, she became very ill with whooping cough. When she was choking one night, Moses Shongo revived her with what we now call mouth-to-mouth resuscitation. After, he told her mother, Blue Flower, "Now she will carry on my work, because my breath is her breath."

True to her grandfather's predictions, Twylah did live in two worlds. Following a childhood of instruction in the Seneca way, and an adolescence of learning both the way of the Native and the non-Native, Twylah married Robert Nitsch, a man of German descent. With their four children, they lived in Buffalo, New York, until the polio epidemic of the 1950s. They moved back then to her

family home and land on the Cattaraugus Reservation, to protect their family. They have lived there since. Robert Nitsch was a successful businessman in the area. Twylah worked for many years as a recreational therapist.

While Twylah never forgot the teachings of her grandfather, nor the responsibilities that they gave her, she was hesitant to discuss them with groups of people. One night, Blue Flower saw Moses Shongo, her brother, and grandmother standing at the foot of her bed. They told her that she had to tell Twylah that it was all right, that she must do the teaching and sharing she was thinking of doing. "She has got to do it," they told Blue Flower. "We have given this knowledge to her, and we are helping her."

Shortly after this experience, Twylah made a tobacco offering in a class that she was teaching, and it felt so right that she opened herself to all of the teachings that were waiting to come through her. Since that time, many people have been opened and enriched by their contact with this understanding and gentle woman.

One of the first things Twylah's pupils learn are four questions that helped the Seneca people to walk always in harmony and balance. They are:

1. Are you happy doing what you are doing?
2. Is what you are doing adding to the confusion?
3. What are you doing to further peace and contentment?
4. How will you be remembered after you are gone—in absence or in death?

These questions can help anyone to evaluate their actions in a way that can bring them into greater harmony with the Earth Mother, and all of their fellow beings. Phrased in a slightly different way, they are a marvelous tool to teach children to take responsibility for their own actions and happiness.

Twylah stresses that to the Seneca, "Self-knowledge was the need, self-understanding was the desire, self-discipline was the way, and self-realization was the goal."

In her book, *Entering into the Silence the Seneca Way,* Twylah writes of how the Seneca learned of himself and nature.

In the very beginning, the early Seneca was drawn close to Nature. Legends related the wonders of Nature and its effects upon all creatures and plants. It was not long before the ancestors of the Senecas sensed a Powerful Force all around them. Everyone saw the results of this Force; some were able to feel it; still others were able to receive impressions from it. They believed it was in everything, everywhere, at all times, for time eternal. They called this Force the Great Mystery and vowed to learn all they could about it.

Legends related that the Indian emerged from the deep and, as he evolved, he increased his awareness by being a student of Nature, recognizing Mother Earth as his caretaker and all creatures of the Great Mystery, his teachers. For this reason, he devoted his life to learning about the secrets that governed Nature. In this way, he began to understand his role in Nature's plan.

Living within the peace and quiet of Nature taught the Indian self-control. He moved slowly, spoke softly, and was habitually silent. Controlled silence was acquired and signified perfect harmony in spirit, mind, body, and action. It was an earned virtue and revered as an honorable trait. To master this trait, the Indian recognized the need for functioning harmoniously in his own environment. His instruction began at an early age and was uniform among all the Indian Nations. There was no need to question the Indian "Way of Life"—it was an accepted fact.

Ancient Seneca instruction introduced a simple but efficient understanding of symbolism. Early routines of daily living revolved around the number four, thus, "4" became a symbolic number and established traditions that held families and Nations together. Its symbolism included the first four Creations, the four stages of learning, the four principles of development, and the four guidelines toward attaining wisdom.

Learning about oneself meant learning how to communicate. One cannot communicate with others unless there is a reasonable amount of self-knowledge, was the belief of the early Senecas.

Communicating means understanding, understanding leads toward peace of mind, peace of mind leads toward happiness, happiness is communicating.

"How well do we communicate?" was the question asked. We learn to measure happiness by the depth of our self-awareness and recognize it by the peace and contentment we enjoy within our environment.

"Entering into the Silence" meant communing with Nature in Spirit, mind, and body. Nature's atmosphere radiated the Spiritual Essence of the Supreme Power and provided the path that led the early Seneca into the "Great Silence."

The legend of the First Messenger tells of the encounter with the Spiritual Essence that was responsible for the practice of "Entering into the Silence."

Two men and two women of great age, honored among their people for their wisdom, sat in the woodlands on the warm earth near a brooklet rippling under a canopy of leaves and branches. They had come to reminisce of their kindred experiences gleaned through their advancing years, when suddenly the heavens opened:

A glorious beam of light,
In all its brilliant splendor,
Gently drifted over them,
Seeding peace and solemnity
On everything it touched.

They watched in wonderment, spellbound by its Sublime Magnificence. It filtered into their bodies, cleansing them throughout, of all infirmities. Presently, they felt themselves being borne aloft to a place of Divine Ecstasy, where the "Secret of the Ages" was revealed, telling them of things to be. They saw the "First Messenger of the Great Mystery," the Spiritual Hand with outstretched fingers and thumb. The message meant, "It comes through." This was the first experience of "Entering into the Silence."

Its symbolism imparts; as the thumb assists the four fingers in life, equality, unity, and eternity, so does the Great Mystery assist all things in Creation. From that time on, the symbolic number "4" became an integral part of the Indian "Way of Life." Following the revelation, the wisdom of the four aged ones increased, and people came from many nations to listen to their Spiritual counseling. From this Divine Experience the entire custom of sitting in Council evolved. It developed that the messengers of the Great Mystery wore many faces. They could be any manifestation in Nature, in creatures, and in earthly forces.

Teaching others how to go into the silence, how to gently walk the pathway of peace is Twylah's lifework, as her grandfather knew it would be. Twylah has also revitalized the Wolf Clan Lodge, and begun the Seneca Indian Historical Society. Through her lecturing, teaching, and writing, Twylah is indeed the voice that rides on the wind. We are happy that she has worked with us in many ways, including being a sacred teacher at many of our Medicine Wheel Gatherings.

Shawnee Goat Clan

Whispering Leaf With Blue Jacket, whose vision appears in Part I, is a brother who has learned to live on Earth Mother in the most simple way. People who came to visit his camp found him and his two children living in wegiwas of simple, local materials. Their brothers and sisters in the plant and animal kingdoms provided their food. The beauty of Earth Mother provided their entertainment and brought them happiness. In time, Whispering Leaf's path has taken him elsewhere. Because of the historical relevance of his clan, we have included this material.

The Goat Clan was organized to be a modern-day warrior society based upon the old ways. Following is their Constitution:

PREAMBLE: The Goat Clan Warrior Society (GCWS) is a small campfire, kindled and nurtured within the hearts of brothers and sisters, which, above all else, seeks to follow the original instructions of the Creation. It is a small family that exists within the larger universal family of mankind. It is a warrior society which seeks through prayer, self-discipline, and simple living to maintain a healthy, happy, and exemplary existence upon the Earth Mother. Toward this goal, it is guided by the following constitution, which was written, not to limit the actions or thoughts, nor to infringe upon basic human rights of people, but to help establish a common path toward self-awareness and discovery of the intimate and eternal link between man and the Great Universal Mystery of Creation.

1. MEMBERSHIP: Membership in the GCWS is offered to all brothers and sisters who are able to embrace the spirit of the Goat Clan and its constitution without undue qualification, and no restriction toward membership shall be placed upon any person because of age, race, or physical effect. All members agree to the following:

   a. To abstain from the consumption of alcohol and/or the use of drugs.
   b. To strive to be a true witness of life by sharing and receiving in a spirit of universal brotherhood without any possessive attachment.

c. To work and live in harmonious union with the forces of Creation, and to exemplify the highest ideals of mind, heart, and spirit.

d. To put the good of the clan, the Tribe, and the Nation above personal ambition, desire, or gain, and to work unceasingly for the renewal of the Sacred Hoop and the healing of our Earth Mother.

e. To walk in a sacred and balanced manner by following the eight guides through daily life. They are: (1) right ideals— universal laws; (2) right motive—love of God; (3) right speech; (4) right action through honesty and truth; (5) right means of livelihood; (6) right effort through self-discipline; (7) right remembrance of the self; (8) right realization—unity with God.

All those persons who are able to embrace the spirit of membership of the GCWS are then eligible for adoption into the clan as a full family member.

2. ADOPTION: Those wishing to be adopted into the Goat Clan may call a special council through the Okema [medicine person]. At this council, each member shall speak for, or against adoption, but adoption shall only be through unanimous decision of all members. Adoption as a full member in the GCWS is accomplished through a sacred, traditional ceremony known as the making of our relatives. During this ceremony the brother or sister, if not in possession of a natural spirit name, will receive one, and thereafter is to be known through this name only, and in keeping with the Great Law of Peace, no question of origin is to arise among clan members.

3. PROPERTY: Since we are of one universal family, and having the same Earth Mother and Sky Father, we will act as true brothers and sisters and share that which has been given to us from the Great Spirit through her children. There will be one cookfire and all will eat together around this fire, sharing whatever food is available. Each member will be given a wooden bowl and spoon for their own continued use. The Clan Mother will be the keeper of common property and will distribute all gifts of bedding, clothing, and cloth material so that each person shall have adequate clothing and bedding to be comfortable and warm during the cold moons. Lodges should be shared whenever possible, and the little ones should be invited to visit all lodges so as to learn of their relationship within the family. The ownership of the lodges rests in the hands of the women. Horses, rifles, bows, knives, shields, medicine bundles, and clothing are to belong to an individual and not to

the clan. The disposition of material gifts to the clan is to be decided upon in general council.

4. The GCWS maintains an open council lodge, and the fire is ever lit. Any member with good cause may call the camp together in special council. The business of the council will be preceded by the silent smoking of the clan pipe, the touching of which will signify that all are pledged to speak the truth. The person then calling the council is given first opportunity to speak. In council, all voices will be equal and all decisions affecting the existence of the camp will be based on unanimous decision of the clan members. Visitors may attend council by invitation, or may call a council through the Okema or Clan Mother to discuss adoption. The Okema will call general council. In addition, the Okema and Clan Mother will maintain an open lodge door for counsel, complaint, suggestion, or discussion at all times.

5. WORK: Much of our original instructions have been forgotten through the loss of essential livelihood. It is through the cultivation of crops that we relearn of the eternal link between man and the sun, moon, rain, and soil. It is through the gathering of nuts and berries, herbs and roots that we are made aware of the bounty spread upon our Earth Mother for our wise use by the Master of Life. It is through the construction of our lodges that we learn the true meaning of shelter, and a respect for our earth home. Because the necessities of food, clothing, and shelter were meant as teachings and not as burdens, all should participate in camp work with willingness to learn how to care and provide for oneself, and to share that knowledge with others who seek to learn. Work should not be divided by age or sex, but should be mutually shared energy for thanksgiving to the Master of Life who sustains us in our every need. Let us share our knowledge, our skills, and our gifts with each other so our work becomes joyous living.

6. INTERACTION WITH DOMINANT SOCIETY: Our Earth Mother is sick, and her children are responsible. For this reason, we of the GCWS have severed ourselves from the day-to-day functions and dependencies of that society. It is our purpose to reestablish the moral, spiritual, and physical environment necessary in order to become instruments of the Great Spirit's will. To this end, we see our work as being contained within the framework of a traditional peoples' village. We do not seek employment for monetary wages, nor will we sell our knowledge, skills, or time. We do not maintain motor vehicles. We seek the life of aboriginals and seek independence from U.S. Government aid in the forms of welfare, food stamps, Medicaid, education, or claims settlements. We do not want our

little ones to be educated by the dominant society. It is our goal to become less dependent on trade goods and more aware of the ecosystem economy in which we live.

7. INTERACTION WITH EARTH MOTHER: All warriors of the Goat Clan must revere and respect the grasses and trees, the waters and sands, the rocks and holy mountains. We must revere and respect all things that live, and all things that do not live: all creatures that walk or crawl, or swim or fly. We must revere and respect the sacred spirit that dwells in all things and beyond all things. With this understanding, we will construct our lodges and shelters with beauty and lightness, using the grasses, reeds, and cane indigenous to our land base. Our lodges will be quonset-shaped wegiwas with frames of cedar saplings and cane. Consumption of food from glass or metal containers that are not reusable should be a terminal practice. Use of petroleum products should be minimized to the maximum possible cutback. We must always remember that the Master of Life is the only real owner of land, and that we are simply caretakers for the unborn generations that will follow us. The land is a sacred trust from Moneto (the Creator) to his children and we do not sell, buy, or rent our Earth Mother or the gifts which grow upon her for the benefit of all creation.

Other People, Clans, and Camps

In Nevada are two traditional camps we know about. One was founded by Rolling Thunder, the well-known Cherokee medicine man, and his late wife, Spotted Fawn, a Shoshone. The other is Frank Thunder's, and consists of a camp and a unique museum. In California is Grandfather Csimu's Red Wind Foundation. These are all traditional camps, with similarities to the Bear Tribe or to the camp of Whispering Leaf.

We have many friends who live in cities but often visit their home places to recharge themselves with the traditional ways. These folks are in the cities to teach others of the way of harmony. Lee Piper, the Bird Clan Mother of the Overhill Band of Cherokees, lives in Seattle and works as minority affairs director of a college there. She actively helps the Native people in the Seattle area, and in her home in the South. Archie Fire, Lame Deer's son, lives outside of Los Angeles and works with people when they are in need of help and medicine. Ernie Peters is also active helping people there, particularly through the sweat lodge.

Crow Dog is a Sioux medicine man who has helped many in the American Indian Movement to return to tradition. He has suffered great harassment from the dominant society because of his work, yet he remains steadfast in the faith. The late Mad Bear was an Iroquois medicine person who had also studied Native religions in many other parts of the world. Osapana Powhatan is a medicine man now living in New Mexico. He has served his people in all the ways he can for many years now.

Gabriel, spoken of in Section Two, is a medicine man who helps people to see more clearly themselves and their relation to the universe. Kwi-tsi-tsa-las is a Kwakiutl medicine woman who runs the Greenvale Herbal College in Canada. Oh Shinnah Fastwolf is an Apache woman who takes the message of the Earth Mother, and her cleansing, to many people via her talks and her music.

Adolf and Beverly Hungry Wolf have shared the traditional Blackfoot message with many people through their series of Good Medicine books.

There are many teachers, both Native and non-Native, who have participated in our Medicine Wheel Gatherings. All of them have shared generously with those attending the Gatherings. The following list honors only some of the teachers who have worked with us. Our thanks go to all of the teachers.

- Grey Antelope is a Tewa Pueblo medicine man, a healer, chanter, and dancer. He has come to the Gatherings with his Humbios Clan Dancers, an interracial group. They have performed the sacred Buffalo, Eagle, Bow, and Corn dances.
- Bear Heart is a Muskogee Indian who trained under two tribal elders and is now a tribal medicine chief. He has Sundanced with both the Northern and Southern Cheyenne people, and is a respected leader in the Native American church.
- Dr. Frans Bakker is the director of the Radiant Life Clinic in California. He is a specialist on rejuvenation health techniques and teacher of radical spiritual healing.
- John Bradshaw of Houston is an educator, theologian, and counselor.
- Dr. Paul Brenner is the author of *Life is a Shared Creation*, and other books. He is the health director for the Center for the Healing Arts, a lecturer, holistic teacher, and physician.
- Tom Brown, Jr., is author of *The Tracker, The Search,* and *The Field Guide to Wilderness Survival.* He is one of the foremost survival instructors and trackers in the world.
- Page Bryant, Sun Bear's first apprentice, is a psychic, radio personality, teacher, and lecturer who teaches the integration

of the psychic and intuitive self. She is the author of several books, including *The Earth Changes Survival Handbook.*

- Red Cloud is a Cree teacher who studied Indian medicine with his grandmother and with Nauskeechask, a noted shaman. He is the former president of the Metis Association of Alberta, Canada.

- Norma Cordell (Eagle Morning Star) is the director of the Eugene (Oregon) Center of the Healing Arts. She is a healer and spiritualist trained by a Nez Perce shaman. She is the author of *Earth Dance.*

- Prem Das is the director of the Mishakai Center for the Study of Shamanism, in northern California. He has studied with the Huichol shaman Don Jose Matsuwa, and is the author of *The Singing Earth.*

- Brooke Medicine Eagle is the great-great-grandniece of Chief Joseph, the Nez Perce holy man and leader. She is trained both in the traditions of her people, and in Western psychology and body work. She lectures throughout the world.

- Evelyn Eaton (Mahad'yuni), who died in 1983, was a pipe woman, healer, and teacher. She was a tribal grandmother to the Bear Tribe. She was the author of *I Send a Voice, Snowy Earth Comes Gliding, The Shaman and the Medicine Wheel,* and twenty other books.

- Wallace Black Elk is a Lakota holy man who has been trained since childhood in the traditional and sacred knowledge of the Earth people. Black Elk has been chosen by the Spirit to be a spiritual guide for all of the people. He is the grandson of the famed Lakota holy man Black Elk, whose vision was shared with the world in *Black Elk Speaks.*

- Oh Shinnah Fastwolf is a Scottish, Apache, and Mohawk eclectic person whose teachings come from various ancient traditions. Oh Shinnah dedicates her work to the healing of Mother Earth.

- Steven Foster and Meredith Little are the founders and former co-directors of Rites of Passage, a teaching organization which guides people along the medicine path. They are now directing the School of Lost Borders in the Owens Valley of California. They co-authored *The Book of the Vision Quest—Personal Transformation in the Wilderness.*

- Adele Getty is a wilderness leader and a ritual consultant who works with reconnecting people with the earth through self-generated ritual.

- Rosemary Gladstar is the founder and director of the California School of Herbal Studies. She is an herbalist, a teacher, and an organizer of holistic health seminars.
- Joan Halifax is the director of the Ojai Foundation in Ojai, California. She is the author of *Shaman: The Wounded Healer*, and *Shamanic Voices*.
- Hawk Little John is a teacher and healer of Cherokee descent. He lectures to many people about the traditional Native ways of healing. He is also a farmer.
- Dr. Elisabeth Kübler-Ross is the director of Shanti Nilaya, a world renowned teacher and lecturer, and a founding member of the American Holistic Medical Association. She is the author of seven books including *On Death and Dying* and *Living with Death and Dying*.
- Winona LaDuke, Sun Bear's daughter, is an internationally known antinuclear activist, and the former director of the Circle of Life Survival School on the White Earth Reservation in Minnesota.
- Barry McWaters, Ph.D., is the co-director of the Institute for the Study of Conscious Evolution and editor of *Humanistic Perspectives*. He is also the author of several books including *Conscious Evolution—Personal and Planetary Transformation* and *The Couple's Journey* (with Susan Campbell).
- Manitonquat (Medicine Story) is a Keeper of the Lore of the Wampanoag people, director of *Another Place* in New Hampshire, founder of the Mettanokit community, and author of *Return to Creation*.
- Norma Meyers is a well-known herbalist and healer of Mohawk descent. She is the director of the Tsonqua Herbal Center in British Columbia, Canada.
- Lee Piper is the Bird Clan Mother of the Eastern Cherokee Overhill Band. She is the author of traditional Native children's stories, a teacher, and a counselor.
- Joan Price works in media, and has presented a slide presentation she developed on Native American sacred areas and the Hopi.
- Starhawk is a ritualist, counselor, writer, and political activist. She is the author of *Dreaming the Dark: Magic, Sex and Politics* and *The Spiral Dance*.
- Brant Secunda has completed his apprenticeship with Don Jose Matsuwa, the Huichol Shaman. He is the ceremonial leader

and director of the Dance of the Deer Foundation: Center for Shamanic Studies.

• Grandfather Sky Eagle is a Chumash teacher and elder.

• The late Grace Spotted Eagle was Wallace Black Elk's wife. She taught about women and the traditional way.

• Brad Steiger is an internationally known author and teacher. He has written *Medicine Power, Medicine Talk, Star People, The Chindi*, and many other books. He is teaching people how to find their multidimensional self.

• Harley Swiftdeer is a Cherokee/Metis medicine man, founder of the Deer Tribe, and teacher of the Sun Dance way, and of White Crystal Medicine.

• Jim Swan is the former director of Life Systems Educational Foundation in Seattle. He is an environmental psychologist specializing in sacred places.

• Slow Turtle (John Peters) is a medicine man for the Wampanoag Nation, and director of Indian Affairs for the state of Massachusetts.

• John White is a well-known teacher, lecturer, and author. He has written many books and edited many anthologies. He is the author of *Pole Shift*.

• Dhyani Ywahoo is the director of the Sunray Meditation Society in Vermont. She is the lineage holder of the medicine traditions of the Anigadoah-Catawaba People, and a Planetary teacher and guide.

• Yehwehnode (She Whose Voice Rides on the Wind), or Twylah Nitsch, speaks with the voice of her ancestors on the wisdom, prophecy, and philosophy of the Seneca people.

• Jack Zimmerman and Jaquelyn McCandless are the focalizers of the Heartlight Community and School outside of Los Angeles. They teach about relationships in the New Age.

These brothers and sisters are helping others to see the light and love of the Great Spirit. They are part of the network of light formed by people of all true traditions that is now covering our Earth Mother, helping to heal her, and to remind us of our connection with the Great Spirit. We are glad to honor them and their work.

IV

Practical
Skills

*In this section Nimimosha, Sun Bear, and
Wabun, with the advice of other Bear Tribe
members—current and past—give solid
suggestions about living on the land, either
alone or in a community.*

Focalizing Community

In the Sixties it was common practice to bask in the illusion that being idealistic was enough to ensure that a utopian new alternative would emerge when people drew together for that purpose. A few realistic individuals dared to differ with that point of view. The idealistic/realistic conflict is still being cultivated in the mainstream, but as we've matured we've seen how counterproductive that is. We were lucky to avoid that pitfall of the angry Sixties, especially lucky in light of the fact that that's when we began all this.

The key word in focalizing community has been *responsibility*. In an attempt to avoid the pitfalls of hierarchy and red tape, many a sincere group has fallen into other pitfalls, particularly that of avoidance. Perhaps it took a try or two before some communities could work. Perhaps experience has allowed a few people to begin again with their eyes wide open. For us, our eyes opened after we were already committed to this vision of an alternative way to live.

Vision is a compelling force. Like any other experience, vision is something already seen, that can never allow you to return to your former world view. We all act upon what we know, upon what life has taught us. Vision is what makes it possible to embark upon a path that is not romantic, not glamorous, not easy, and has none of the rewards we are taught to value. The rewards of community are personal growth, vision, greater courage, creativity, and joy in life. Joy in nurturing life. Joy in participating in life. Joy in all aspects of life. Few of us were taught the maturity required to value these things adequately.

Focalizing community can be thought of as a "thankless task," although it isn't, once we let go of old attitudes about freedom versus commitment, work versus happiness, risk versus security, responsibility versus fun. You will, at times, work more hours than you ever thought a person could. You will cover work left undone by people you thought you could rely on. You will take risks, not just for yourself, but for your whole community, and you will bear the strain of the unknown outcome. You will make a few unpopular decisions, and feel the resentment of people in whose interest you are acting. Others will expect you to manifest the changes they want, and come up with the money for things they regard as important. You will be called upon to do tasks too difficult or complicated for anyone else. You will not always have enthusiastic response to your need for help.

You will be unpopular when you make people face unpleasant facts. You will sometimes doubt your own perception, especially when, in spite of your total commitment to doing your best, things aren't going well. You will feel inadequate when the cash flow isn't flowing. You will feel loneliness when you perceive that others cannot or will not be individually or adequately motivated, experienced, educated, or wise to give you the relief you feel you need. You then ask yourself exactly why you hang in there, still praying, still looking within, still loving the task you've set out to do.

The answer must be that your work is important, and that it is your path.

Having What It Takes

Shared purpose is the only reason for having a community. Shared purpose is important before anything else. Purpose is more important than having a home together, or having land, or sharing your knowledge and experience, or having money. This purpose must be strong, and shared truly from deep within. This purpose must be able to survive difficult times, times of doubt, times of careful self-examination. Shared purpose is so important that we are compelled to express it as clearly as possible to each other, and to know, not assume, agreement.

The Tribe has a written statement of purpose. This statement changes as our purpose becomes larger, and as our vision grows. Our purpose is alive, not rigid and unchanging. This reality reflects our growth at all levels. All of us have participated in stating our written purpose.

One of the most important things that a stated purpose gives, especially in the early growth of a community, is a guideline by which to make decisions. It makes it possible to answer such questions as, what decision will be in harmony with our vision and purpose? Are we serving our purpose? Later, it helps new people know whether or not they belong in your community. It becomes a guideline by which to discriminate between what is essential and what is disruptive. Ultimately, when the world knocks on your door to question your departure from the American Dream, you will have a way to explain yourself, and you and your community will be able to present an example of agreement, unity, and shared priority.

Positive Attitude

Three attitudes work well toward achieving a positive, constructive community: wanting to do (not just achieve) the work of building community, believing in this work as life-affirming and good, and knowing that it's possible for you to do. Seeing the larger picture of your relationship to the world is immeasurably valuable, and vital. It does much to dispel loneliness and the illusion of separation from other people, and from the world.

Regardless of your stated purpose, your activities and lifestyle will have an impact on the world in some way. The people in your community are directly affected by it, and they, in turn, touch others with their individual energies. Your community energy will have its impact on the immediate environment and on the neighborhood or local area. Simple activities like recycling, protecting wildlife habitat, growing a garden, all have far-reaching effects just as much as harmful activities do. You are part of Creation, and it is an illusion to pretend that you are somehow above it or separate from it.

Listening

Listening is one of the lost arts. It was a part of the recent enough past, however, that we are able to retrieve it. Among the Native American people, the elders were listened to in a way that's hard to explain. In modern America, we learn to listen shallowly, enough to memorize facts, or to detect points we want to refute, or enough to make someone feel respected, as duty requires. So often we listen to the words but not the message. We hear the notes but not the music, see the lines but not the art. It is truly our loss that we cannot see anew through the eyes of another.

There are two kinds of listening that are essential in a community: listening to the voice of spirit, and listening to the voice of individual and collective need within the community. When members learn to listen, both they and the community experience miraculous growth.

Discrimination

No one community can be all things to all people. Learning what you reasonably can and cannot do is essential, and difficult. Many people coming to community want to change everything in their lives at once. This doesn't work. To survive and prosper a community needs to limit itself, and be clear about its limits. Members need to learn to say a rational "no" to new goals or projects that could overwhelm them, to unsought advice, and to potential members who are not in harmony with their purpose.

Land

There are many ways to get land. The Bureau of Land Management puts land up for sale. These are cash deals, but reasonable. Contact the office for the area in which you are interested. Mining claims can also be useful to some people. You can stake a claim on twenty acres of public land, providing you can prove that there are minerals there. Sometimes you can get the use of existing mining claims by looking after them for the owners. You can also camp in national forests on a temporary basis, and on Bureau of Land Management land, but you cannot put up any permanent shelters. Of course, if you have the money, there are a lot of deals available through private parties. In this case, it is best to scout the area you are interested in. Sometimes people have land they bought for speculation or to retire on and they will let you live on it. Check on property taxes. Check everything.

In looking at land, remember that the water supply is very important. Be sure you have a pure water supply for drinking, and a steady supply for animals and irrigation. If you have to have a well put in, it could cost you $5,000 or more. Check on local land restrictions as to septic tanks, or whether they'll let you get by with an outhouse.

In the past we were involved in acquiring land in many of the ways mentioned above.

We thought of land as something to use, but not to own. We felt that ownership of the Earth Mother should only be vested in the Great Spirit. During past years we used land, but didn't own it. This way was successful when we dealt with people with true hearts and spirits. When we dealt with some who spoke with forked tongues, they made it impossible for us to continue using land that we did not own.

Several times, we have put much energy and money into someone else's land, and buildings we created on it, only to find that the owners had both forked tongues and crooked hearts. We had to move on at their whim.

In the fall of 1975, we decided that to have a stable land base during this time of change, we would have to purchase land ourselves. We felt the need to be the "legal" owners, according to the customs of this society, of the land we would be caring for. At this time, we felt this would be the only way we could bring some land, and our lives, into the balance that we feel is necessary.

So we went in search of land. We knew that we wanted to be in the foothills of the Rocky Mountains. We wanted land with a natural water supply, and with areas where we could raise a garden, keep some chickens, and pasture goats or a milk cow. We wanted an area that was isolated, yet accessible by road.

We found that realtors have an odd language that they use in newspaper ads. "Reasonable" in 1975 could mean anything from $350 to $1,500 per acre. "Gently sloping" seemed to describe land that is accessible only in the summer, and then only in a four-wheel drive vehicle. "Good water" often meant that the water would be good if you could afford to drill 150 feet down for a well.

When looking for land, you must consider all of these things, and more. Generally, in 1987, well drilling costs at least $30 per foot. Bringing power in costs at least $2 per foot, and you may have to sign a $20-per-month minimum contract for a five-year period. You must also check out legal access that allows you to drive in and out, utilities, zoning laws, the building code, and how much houses will cost. It's sad that it is this way, but true, and as long as this system exists, we feel better about complying with its laws than about getting caught up in its court system because the foundation of our house isn't proper.

The medicine was good to us again, and we found some beautiful acreage within our price range. It has a natural spring, two ponds, pasture, trees, and wilderness for the back yard. Wild fruit and herbs abound, there are fishing streams nearby, and we've seen tracks of deer, coyote, and elk. To us, the spring was very important, since if you have only a well, you are usually dependent on electricity to pump the water.

One day, we know, the land will be free to those who would live on it in harmony with the way of the Great Spirit. Until then, it is sometimes good to follow the example of our brothers, the fox and coyote, and to move further from the cities, back in the brush and silent land.

Shelters

The kind of shelter you need depends on climate, water supply, available materials, and how long you plan to be in one place. Following is a listing of different shelters, and our suggestions.

Brush Lean-to

This is made of a basic frame of poles or stripped branches, and covered with brush, grass thatching, or reeds. This gives shade and some protection from wind. A little canvas or plastic adds protection from rain and snow.

Tipi or Tent

The tipi was used a lot by the Plains Indians. Theirs were made of heavy buffalo hides and had liners in them. The modern canvas

One of the Bear Tribe tipis

ones are all right for warm climates, but we wouldn't recommend them for wintering in cold areas. If you buy or make a tipi, make sure that it's waterproof or waterproof it yourself. We recommend tipi living because it helps people experience the sacred circle of life. We only point out one disadvantage of the tipi, and that is that it sticks out and shows up for miles in most country, which isn't helpful if you're trying to be inconspicuous.

Wickiup

These begin with a framework of poles anchored in the ground and bent over and lashed to form a small dome. At this stage the wickiup looks like a bare sweat lodge. Other poles can be added horizontally. Many Eastern Woodland tribes laced on birch bark, but bark and other materials can be used. A layer of plastic or canvas under the covering will keep things a lot cleaner inside.

Earth Lodge

This type of dwelling is suitable in places where it isn't too rocky or rainy. One type is dug into the earth three or four feet, with two or three feet of wall above ground, then a roof added. These blend nicely into a wilderness background. Other dwellings can be built out of sod, like the ones built by the settlers on the prairies where money and materials were short. Strips of sod were arranged like bricks to make a house that was warm in winter and cool in summer. Rammed earth also makes blocks suitable for building, but it should be carefully done and tested before it is relied upon to hold up in severe weather. The same is true of adobe blocks. These must be cured for at least two weeks, and are best used in mainly dry climates.

Log Cabin

A sturdy cabin can be built with reasonable effort in areas where the materials are available. Logs of uniform size need less hewing to match them. Notching is very important as the notches take the place of nails. They must line up. Cured logs should be used for any permanent dwelling. Green ones may crack, ooze pitch, warp, and do all kinds of things. Cracks between the logs can be chinked with a number of materials, from mud to sod to concrete.

Roofs are difficult because of all the lifting needed. The main roof beams should be one pole, strongly fixed to the walls. The pitch of the roof will depend on what kind of weather it must withstand. A good framework is important for supporting the roof. It is wise to inspect roofs of other structures before you decide how to build yours. A number of materials can be used to cover the basic framework, such as slab wood, birch bark, thatching. Be sure to think in advance of such things as water resistance and insulation. Sometimes these are more easily incorporated in the building than added later.

Log cabins are attractive for their lasting value, and for the builder's independence from lumber mills. They are, however, quite work-intensive. It is a long process to select and fell trees, and the work of stripping off the bark and waiting for the logs to cure is a major test of patience. It's satisfying to complete one of these when the shelter harmonizes with the surrounding terrain, is solid, and needs no paint or siding.

Rock House

For someone who has the time, rock construction is good. It's lasting and it has beauty. It's fire resistant and never needs to be painted. Some people combine rock with other materials. A small investment in mortar is necessary, and a good foundation.

Domes

These are good, cheap housing. Our objection is that without good maintenance they quickly become an eyesore. Dome kits can be bought, or you can follow a plan and build out of wood.

House

The Bear Tribe lives in a large house (twenty-four feet by sixty-four feet with an addition, two-story), built by our own people. It is mainly built out of materials considered to be of inferior quality, and we got them free or cheap. If you can salvage, recycle, scrounge, bargain, and improvise, you might get what you need within a very limited budget. This means you may have to consider using materials you had not considered before. We've always been willing to combine standard materials with others we find. The materials we find fall into two basic groups—natural materials like rock (also very labor-intensive and not very warm) and wood (for cabinet handles, towel racks and curtain rods, table legs, etc.) and substandard building supplies like salvaged siding, insulation, fixtures, doors, windows, stairs, and discarded materials which were warped, splintered, or odd sizes.

There are a number of factors to consider when you select materials. If you want a house that will look clean when you've cleaned it—not dingy—and be easy to take care of, you will have to be more selective about wall and floor coverings. Bare, natural wood is very nice when it's new, but once it's stood a while, it tends to absorb dust and smoke to shower down upon your dining

The Bear Tribe's longhouse under construction

room table at a later time. The amount of attention paid to detail (such as finishing a garment you have made) will make a great deal of difference in the feeling of quality of the dwelling. The same applies to outbuildings—woodsheds and tool sheds. If you take the time to hang the doors right, they will always open and shut.

When we first built the longhouse at Vision Mountain, we had little money, a newborn infant, animals and gardens that needed immediate attention, business to attend, a tiny work force, and a limit of twenty-four hours in a day. Because of our circumstances, we needed a home, cheap and in a hurry. We cut lots of corners in cost and construction. We did live to regret some of the decisions we made. We now wish we had a home with washable walls, insulation in the subfloor, more windows. However, we avoided perpetual debt. We own the place, and we have been able to add a wing and lift part of a roof. We could do it because we understood (by then) how building components go together, and how ours was built.

We've found that it's hard to overestimate your needs in terms of space. While it's true that a smaller dwelling is easier and cheaper to heat, we have found that we sometimes have insufficient work space for all projects—baking bread, beadwork, canning the garden, sewing, office work, carving, music, holding programs, and ordinary activities. On the one hand, we did underestimate future space needs. On the other hand, we didn't overbuild and overbudget.

Floor plans must take into account the immediate needs of the group, and individual needs for privacy. If there are children, there must be room in your home for them. Comfort and cleanliness are so important that we stress the need to acquire some experience in building, or research it well, at least. Insulate well. Allow for circulation of oxygen. Yet budget realistically. It is a good idea to write two budgets, one you hope to adhere to, and another showing the cost of building the traditional way. Be prepared to pay the bill either way. This will allow you to change your mind about floor coverings, for instance. Furthermore, if you are unprepared to foot the bill, your project will be interrupted when it is partially done. Any house left unoccupied always ages badly, compared to an occupied dwelling. It is important to get the house liveable.

Safety is another important aspect of building—both during the work of building with power tools, and long distances to fall, and after the building is complete. Your research into wood stoves, for instance, should occur before you build. You need sufficient clearance for even the safest metalbestos roof packs, and you absolutely must check on insurance and fire marshal regulations. Then you will build according to your needs, and not have to change things later.

Carefully check local building codes and electrical codes before beginning the construction of your house. Begin with a good foundation, literally, and in terms of information. Most of the time, you can build your house with no hassle from the county if you simply buy a building permit and adhere to the county guidelines. They only want your fee, and they want to know how to assess the value of your property so they can tax it. Our longhouse was designated a ''low-quality dwelling,'' and our taxes are very low.

Anything you want in your house is easier to do in the first place, if you can afford it. Additionally, you need to look at the surrounding terrain to see if there are things you need to do to protect your house. Do you need rain gutters? Do you need to build a little earth berm to keep rainwater from flooding your kitchen?

The electrical codes will be much more strict, and for good reason. Poor wiring causes many tragic fires. If your mind fails to comprehend this code, don't hesitate to get help from a friend you *know* can do it. The power company will *not* hook you up until everything is according to their specifications. Additionally, insurance companies take a dim view of insuring anything at all, especially if it doesn't look "right." Quality in this respect is absolutely essential.

We feel it is wise to have an alternative to electric heating even if you equip your house for that. We heat with wood. One centrally located stove heats almost the entire house. We built the house with space around the stairs so that the heat from the downstairs effectively heats the second story. Again, the word is *safety*. We can't emphasize it enough. Buy fire extinguishers. Keep flammables far away from fires.

Other Hints

There are any number of excellent books available from libraries which show the detail of building traditional or alternative shelters. It is well worth the time spent to read ten or twelve books on building—you are thinking about making a major investment in time and money (counting transportation, materials, time off from work), and you can't afford many mistakes. If you do make mistakes, take the time to correct them, rather than covering them up or hoping it isn't very important. You want to have a house that will bear the weight of whatever roofing you have, and snow, and solar water heating, or whatever will be going on your roof.

When you pick a location for your dwelling, be sure to consider your water source, access (for purposes of bringing in electricity; phone, if desired; supplies; wood; food), fire danger, beauty, climate, and safety from possible flooding. It is good to have an overall plan for your home or community, with projected sites for outhouse, woodshed, barn, root cellar, gardens, well, or springhouse. This can save a lot of steps in daily chores, and also avoid mistakes such as putting an outhouse too close to a water source.

Interior

In a permanent house, beauty and comfort are as important as function, and they tie in together. An organized area will automatically be more attractive and appear larger than an unplanned one. But you also have to think about such things as light and warmth, cleanliness, and color. All these things can contribute much to your happiness and energy for other things. Here are some of the things we have found helpful.

Plan the kitchen. The kitchen, or the hearth, is the center of the home. It reflects the condition of the family. Its condition is also reflected in the family. The food which nourishes us is prepared here.

Cleanliness is of utmost importance. Plan where you want

your water supply to be kept. Go to adequate measures to get good containers for it. Where will you dispose of used water? Where will you stack dirty dishes? Where will you keep the clean ones? Take the time daily to keep your house clean. People who live in pig-pens often act like pigs.

It is good to organize firewood so that it is near the door and near (but not too near) the stove. There should be adequate space so that wood can be dried out if necessary.

The cook stove will be the center of the kitchen on hot days as well as cool, so plan accordingly. It is where food is canned and cooked, where water is heated for all hot water needs (unless you plan to have electric, gas, or solar equipment), and where people will go to thaw out.

If there will be stoves in other parts of the house, designate places for firewood. Build boxes for it. Make it easy to use. Plan for ease in housekeeping, and for beauty. Curtains, plants, flowers,

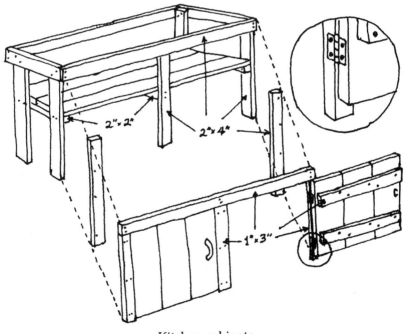

Kitchen cabinets

attractive furniture—purchased or homemade—make a big difference in how the house looks and how you feel living in it. Carpeting or linoleum brightens a house up and helps to insulate.

Adequate light is crucial, especially in the winter. Plan to have sufficient windows, and good lighting from electric or other sources. We strongly recommend *not* having fluorescent bulbs as they tend to agitate people.

Furniture and cabinets are more a necessity than a luxury, as you will quickly learn when times get busy. It is wise to plan your projected needs, then custom build for versatility. If you need temporary kitchen shelves, build them shallow enough to serve later as a bookcase, or deep enough to use as pantry shelves or linen storage. Wasting work is as bad as wasting materials. You can build cupboards a lot cheaper than buy them, and they are more attractive. The inside of cabinets is a simple shelf, which can be built into the wall. For nice-looking cabinets use facer boards that match the doors and produce an even surface. Obtain good hinges and latches.

Refer to the sketch on page 103 of the kitchen cabinets we use in the longhouse. Remember that cupboards are essential if you have toddlers in the family.

Plan for adequate storage and closet space. We've found that a loft bed about five feet high is a good bedroom space saver, as your closet and dressers can go underneath.

Water

Having your own water source is a blessing. Daily prayers to the spirits that guard it are important.

Before you buy land with a well or spring it is good to test for any toxic materials that may have polluted it. Either test it yourself or have it tested through the county. The fee will be reasonable. In any case, it will be more reasonable than an illness caused by drinking contaminated water. If you have a stream, find out what is upstream that could get into the water. If you have a well or a spring, maintain it. We drain our wood spring box once or twice a year and use a spray containing a bleach that has sodium hypochlorite as its only active ingredient. We also cover it with screen in the summer, as it seems more effective than a wood top in keeping insects out. We always ask permission of the spring spirit before making changes.

Contamination is the worst threat to water storage. Realize that *anything* added to water reduces its quality. This includes material from the container or reservoir. Invest whatever is required to protect your water supply. It's impossible to live without an adequate supply of good water.

Changes in weather and season sometimes affect the quantity and quality of water. Become familiar with the lay of the land and how it relates to the water supply.

We try to use water sparingly, and for as many uses as it will stand. Become aware of all the uses water is put to, like drinking, cooking, bathing, livestock, gardening, cleaning, canning, dishwashing, house plants, etc. Most people use more water than they think for all these. It is good standard practice to use as little as possible for everything.

Alternatives to using a lot of water for bathing are bathing in a basin most of the time, or using a sauna or sweat lodge. Gardens can be irrigated with the runoff from other projects, if there are no foreign substances in the water. Laundry should be done only when necessary. Let the sun freshen your out-of-season clothing. Use less soap and less rinse water. Do more than one load of clothing in wash water.

If you are lucky and have enough water for a system, decide what your needs will be over a projected period.

Can you have a gravity flow system? This is best if you can. Otherwise, is electric power dependable in your area? Do you plan to use a pump in your well? If so, try to design it so you can also dip water.

Make sure you take steps in warm weather to keep all your water from freezing when it's cold. This means burying any hose or pipe below the frost line and insulating it with straw or insulation and soil. Use the best quality pipe you can afford. Cheap pipes spring leaks in about five years.

If you decide to install plumbing, be sure you have enough water to make it practical and be sure you take measures to prevent freezing, or your system will be destroyed and you will lose many gallons of water through burst pipes. Keep track of the amount of water being used. A common result of having plumbing is that people use more water, as it is easier to get.

Part of our economy is looking at the ways we use water. At Vision Mountain, we have some of the best water that exists. Because the spring is located in such a magic-feeling place we were immediately aware of what a sacrament it is. We have been unwilling to dishonor it by using it stupidly. In the days when we had to carry every drop, we made sure the water was used first for dishes, then for a few very dirty clothes, then for floors. We learned to bathe in six quarts of water, which sufficed for washing hair first. Now that we have gravity-flow water into the house, we find we still don't take that gift for granted. We use it more generously, yes. We take an occasional therapeutic bath in a tub, and we drain dishwater when it has been thoroughly used. We still flush only when necessary, though. We don't take clean drinking water for washing the floor.

A good wringer washer is an excellent way to make more honest use of water. We use an automatic washer now, with justifications we feel all right about, but we use a machine that has a water level control. It still wastes some water, but not as much as other machines. We use a clothesline instead of a dryer whenever we can.

A little hard work gives good perspective on water. When our youngest child was an infant we discovered, counting the price of cloth diapers, laundry soap, quarters for laundromat machines and dryers, pins, pails, pants, we still saved $700 per child by using

cloth diapers instead of disposable ones. This means we washed cloth ones. First we split firewood, then found a bucket with a handle to go get water. We had a hand-operated wringer washer. We could adjust our own temperature according to how much wood we were willing to split, give the paddle 100 churns, run the diapers through the wringer, and drop them into the pot of rinse water, then use the sudsy water for the next round of diapers. It was a heck of a lot of work. It was worthwhile for reasons at two levels: one, water was in limited supply and was needed everywhere on the farm; and two, it gave us perspective about how water was handled in the good old days when there was plenty of water. It helps us appreciate the peoples of the Third World countries who must carry their water many miles for drinking and cooking.

Following are some suggestions for conserving water:

1. Keep a jar of water in the refrigerator so people won't run the faucet just to get a cool drink.
2. Showers use less water than baths.
3. On-off showers where you wet yourself down, shut off the water, soap up, and then turn on the water to rinse off use even less. Water-saving devices within the shower head, and on-off buttons on the shower save even more water.
4. Flush only when necessary. Be sure your fixtures are working properly, not leaking.
5. If you have a reservoir-type toilet, put a quart bottle or a brick in the tank and you'll use less each time you flush.
6. Wash only clothing which is dirty. Automatic washers are wasteful. Wash some things by hand.
7. Do not use harsh or chemical cleaning agents—soaps like Ivory are the gentlest and are better for the Earth Mother than detergents.
8. Recycle water. Use dish rinsing water for another job, like washing the floor or an article of clothing.

9. Don't let the water run while you are shaving or brushing your teeth.
10. Find some way to catch rainwater (barrels under the rain gutters is one). This can be used for washing and watering.
11. Keep plumbing in good repair.
12. Give up your lawn and grow vegetables.
13. Water your garden by hand. Don't walk away and leave water running. Don't water driveways.

Waste

You will need a way to dispose of human and kitchen waste without defiling the portion of the Earth Mother given into your care. For human waste you may use an outhouse, a composting toilet, a methane-producing toilet, an incinerating toilet, or a toilet hooked into a septic system. Digging holes isn't realistic for a group of people on a permanent land base. We've seen some good plans for methane and composting toilets, but they aren't practical with the number of people we have. You need propane for incinerating toilets. We've chosen to have an outhouse and a septic system.

We make sure the outhouse is away from any water or gardens. We use ashes from our stoves and lye in the summer to keep the outhouse fresh. We move it every four to six months depending on the number of people here. To build a septic system you need the proper permits and a backhoe or a lot of time. You also need the tank and gravel and straw for the leach lines. To have a system installed costs at least $1,500, materials and labor considered.

Unless you are sure of your water supply's abundance, a septic system isn't a good investment. Without adequate water to keep the system moving, the septic tank turns into an accidental methane generator that is unpleasant to have around.

Although a septic system is the most responsible way of disposing of kitchen waste water (which often should not be used on plants because of dirt or grease or detergents), you can just throw dirty water on an arid area such as a driveway, and use whatever water you can recycle on plants or trees. Do use biodegradable cleansers and be cautious, as even some of these harm trees and plants.

Recycling

Another important aspect of disposing of waste products is recycling. Recycling is more than taking cans, paper, and glass to a recycling center. It is an attitude of boycotting the consumerism addiction of most people. It is recycling your thoughts so you don't need to buy a new coat or appliance just because it's on sale. Real recycling is realistic economics. Group recycling activities and large weekend projects have their important place, but recycling is for every day. Anyone who survived the Great Depression of the thirties can tell you all about it.

Most recycling is still done by individuals who turn scraps into quilts, cans into flowerpots, or garbage into compost. Ironically, in some circles these same conscientious people become targets of criticism from others who consider them lax for using disposable diapers one weekend or having an electric heater to supplement their wood heat. Yet these are some of the people who usually do more recycling than any commercial industry has yet attempted to do.

We advocate that everyone begin a daily recycling program that is realistic for their own lifestyle—a pattern that they can continue to improve upon—rather than an enormous project which they can't ever hope to maintain. The following suggestions are only a few ideas. Select the ones that are useful to you.

Shopping

Things cost so much these days that most of us need to be selective about what we buy new and what we buy secondhand. When buying used items, you don't pay for advertising, brand name, and style. Being able to find good deals is a skill worth developing, and buying this way is often a lot of fun.

Thrift stores and garage sales are good places to find used items. Children's items which are quickly outgrown can usually be found cheaply and in good condition. New luggage is expensive, so if you seldom go on trips, a thrift store is a good place to shop for it. Eyeglass frames are ridiculously expensive, but in a thrift store they can often be bought for less than a dollar.

Rummage sales are a good place to shop if you get there early, but most of the bargains will be snapped up in the first hour. Get there early, examine all items carefully, and wash them before you use them. Try out appliances to be sure they work and will continue to work.

The dump is usually the last place to look for things you need. Yet many horse-watering troughs have been picked up there.

Washing machines may still have good motors worth money. Just be wary of the filth that accompanies anything from the dump. Classified ads list goods and equipment of all kinds. Many of these items must be left behind when people move. Bankruptcy auctions are usually listed in the legal column. Watch for them. Reselling your own unused articles is also important. Turning an unused piano into a washing machine is financially and aesthetically sound.

Around the House

We can learn through separating the garbage what it is we can do as "only one person" for our environment and our economy. We have recycled aluminum as well as we could. Surprisingly, we found that the recycling center was not interested in foil. The center was interested in cans only, and in aluminum siding, enamel and all, if the nails are pulled out.

If you balk at paying outrageous prices for food storage containers that quickly stain and split at the corners, you can save cottage cheese and yogurt containers for other foods. If you make your own dairy products you can collect containers from your friends. They may be good for only a few uses, but they work, and more containers can be accumulated at no additional cost. Plastics are products of the petroleum industries, and they are not biodegradable. They do not readily melt down to be remade into other things. Their fumes are toxic. It therefore behooves us to use all plastics for as long as we can. Even us plastics-haters should be taking care of the plastics that already exist, so that fewer will need to be manufactured later to supply consumer habits. Yes, it will take some time and energy, and it will use some space. However, it is a far greater thing to recycle than it is to throw up our hands in despair over the brutalization of earth by industry.

Separating the trash is basic, but requires space. Household garbage can be separated into meat and grease for dogs and cats; vegetable scraps for chickens, pigs, and rabbits; compost; paper; and plastic for the dump. Paper, glass, and cans should be taken to a recycling center.

Saving containers saves money. Plastic bags are the first things we save. We use them for dried foods, homemade bread and rolls, covering leftovers, shoe bags, and many other things. Paper bags are natural for reuse. Milk cartons are good pots for tomato seedlings and other plants which must be started indoors. They are also good for freezing fish and other food in large amounts, or block ice. Large cans are easily converted into flowerpots or canisters (coffee cans are the best). Baking powder and cocoa cans are useful in a

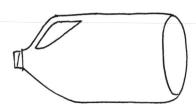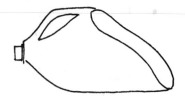

How to make a scoop from a plastic bleach jug

workshop or sewing area. Spice jars work neatly for buttons, beads, hair pins, and other odd stuff. Large jars can be used for food storage when metal is not advisable, and smooth-edged cans can be used for feeding dogs and cats. Almost any container has possibilities, and as long as we pay so dearly for packaging, we should get as much mileage from it as we can.

We have been able to use every kind of fabric scrap, from nylon to canvas to fake leather. We've made quilt tops, pot holders, pin cushions, lampshades, toys, slippers, pouches, and we've used the tiny snips for stuffing. Again, the possibilities are endless.

Newspapers are a valuable resource. They start fires, wrap dishes for storage, mulch gardens, cushion items for mailing, and housebreak puppies. They catch spills, insulate, clean up. Don't throw them away.

Dog food bags have insulation qualities and are strong. Egg boxes can be used for sound and temperature insulation. Scraps of rug, linoleum, or tile are valuable in pet or doorway areas.

Leftovers in the kitchen should always be reheated for another meal. Left-over leftovers are a harder problem, but they can be managed.

Worn out sheets and towels can be a real lifesaver if they are clean. Finding enough rags for odd jobs or emergencies (slings and such) can be a challenge. They are good for all kinds of equipment maintenance, and for draping clothing in storage. Always useful for cleaning, they are also good to keep in a vehicle for cleaning windows, checking oil, and for mopping up spills.

Most farm people are great recyclers who find uses for vegetable parings, egg shells, coffee grounds, ashes, and soap chips. We find that getting the most out of everything will cut down the shopping list.

Outdoors

Outdoors, there's plenty of opportunity to recycle junk that is otherwise an eyesore and maybe even a hazard. Discarded scrap iron can be added to rusty baling or fencing wire and used for stabilizing concrete. This is done by pouring the cement over all this junk right in the form.

Used motor oil can be used for a number of things. It can be used with a worn-out paintbrush for conditioning hooves. It can be used for oiling a very dusty driveway, for preventing rot on fence-posts, or for weed control around a pumphouse, so long as it can do no harm to animals or water source. Do *not* try to use it on leather.

Manure from livestock should be collected and used. It is far better than chemical fertilizer and is very expensive if you have to buy it. Leaves and wet straw which can't be used for animal bedding, and lawn clippings can all be composted or used in a garden as mulch. Mulching cuts back the growth of weeds, and therefore insects, and it conserves moisture.

Sawdust makes good insulation where some temperature control is important. Feed sacks can be reused for insulation, fire control, and other things. Ashes can be sprinkled on icy paths.

Many of these recycling ideas will be useful and convenient for you. You doubtless have ideas of your own.

Wood

Over the years, we've used a great deal of wood for the construction and heating of our homes. This brings to us the awareness that we therefore share some of the responsibility to care for our trees and forests. These particular plant people have protected us from exposure to the elements, kept us comfortable, fueled our ceremonial fires, cooked our food. These trees also provided beauty to the land where we live, showed us where to find water, freshened the air, shaded us, and provided a natural windbreak. They sheltered the animals here, both wild and domestic. We therefore feel that we must take a role in caring for whatever part of the forest we can, by removing fire hazards, using safe practices with our fires, and being thankful for whatever we take. We pause to be thankful, make a prayer, leave tobacco when we take the dead relatives of the plant people for our own use.

On a more mundane level, we have also become more aware of the real cost of firewood. Even if we pick up slash for our use, it isn't "free." We must count the costs of driving a truck (the cost goes much further than the price of the gasoline), buying and running a chainsaw, building a woodshed, acquiring permits when those are needed, and the human costs of time and energy.

Remember wood is not an unlimited resource. Nor should trees be treated merely as fuel. They are fellow beings and should be treated with respect. Thank them for giving themselves so you can be warm and continue to live. Continue showing respect by having adequate arrangements to maintain and contain your fire area.

Prevention of spreading fire is a major consideration. Have a fire extinguisher near every stove or fireplace, even if it is only a five-gallon container of water that is easy to reach. Do not try to camouflage it because of its appearance. Learn to accept it. Do not pile things on it. Check it often to be sure it is available and full, and workable, if it is a regular fire extinguisher. Be sure you know

114

how to open or use it. And don't hesitate to use it the minute fire gets out of hand.

If you are heating with wood, search out your area and find good, fallen dead timber. Never cut green wood unless you absolutely must, and you are prepared to let it dry for about six months to cure it, as it will not burn green. Gathering dead trees gives both you and the forest extra fire protection. A bow saw or buck saw is your best bet for a camp wood supply. Also get a single- or double-bit axe or a small sledge hammer and wedge. Hatchets are okay only for boy scouts and weekend campers. If you're going into the woods for permanent living, you should have a minimum wood supply for two weeks ahead. Cut out the dead timber near your camp first, then fan out.

You will need to keep your wood dry. Properly stacked wood will stay fairly dry, but it is better to put up a woodshed—just a simple roof on four posts will do in a pinch. Even a tarp or plastic sheet helps a lot.

You will find that different wood burns differently. All wood is usable for burning in the day. But small pieces burn quickly and need to be replaced often. Some kinds of wood burn hot and fast—others burn long and evenly. You will learn what kind you prefer for what purpose. Some people burn pine in the daytime when they are there to restoke the stove, but burn tamarack at night so the house will stay warm. It is important to find out what woods are plentiful in your area, and where to look for dead trees. In a house where wood is the only fuel, a great deal of wood is burned over one winter. Estimate your needs from the experience of others, and by scrutinizing your own needs and the size of your home. It's better to overestimate, rather than underestimate.

Keep flammable things well away from the fire area—like rugs, coats, wet laundry, chairs, bedding, toys, and above all, flammable liquids and vapors. Keep firewood in its own container, and make sure the wood can't slide down against the side of the stove. Do not let children play in the area. Plan your traffic pattern through the house with safety in mind.

Have adequate equipment for cleaning stoves, and clean stoves and chimneys often. Caked-on soot is the usual cause of roof fires. Chimneys must be clean in order to draw well, and stoves full of ashes do not work. In the winter, cleaning ashes will need to take place every two or three days. In the summer, it will be less often.

Under no circumstances leave a fire unattended. Open fireplaces are charming, but are less practical than a stove which can be banked for long burning with relative safety, and can be used for many needs.

In fireplaces, always use a screen to keep flying sparks in the fire area. Don't encourage children to feed any fire. Wood stoves should not be placed too close to walls or furniture. Cover walls in these areas with a fireproof material.

When camping, always clear a large area around your fire, clear down to the mineral earth. Put your fire out at night. Never burn quantities of paper in an open fireplace, as burning paper easily flies out.

Never start any fire by using gasoline or oil.

When using a chain saw or motorcycle in the woods or brush, be sure it is equipped with a spark arrestor, and watch it. Never smoke while walking in the woods.

Fire is a wonderful friend, but an uncontrolled fire is one of man's and Mother Earth's worst enemies.

Vegetables

The gardener's basic attitude toward the earth, his plants, and himself as a gardener, and about his garden as a whole, all have a definite effect on the growth and productivity of the garden.

Respect for the Earth Mother herself is very important. When you first begin your garden and start to develop the land, explain to the spirits of the area why you break the earth, kill the weeds, and why you are disturbing the natural balance of the area.

The individual plants of the garden deserve respect as well, for they work hard to produce a crop for you. Respect for the plants entails attention throughout the growing season. Plants should be checked for parasites, for moisture, and for whether they need cultivation. Many gardeners have a tendency to plant their crops, water, and otherwise leave them to struggle along on their own until the crop is ready. Another thing you must remember is that all the crop must be used, because it is disrespectful to the individual plant, the species, and the garden as a whole to waste any part of the crops yielded. If you can't handle the abundance of your garden, sell or give the excess to someone who can.

Thinning and weeding is attention plants need. Some gardeners fear thinning plants as they don't want to kill them. Plants need space, however, to produce their best. Without space to grow, they are subject to disease, parasites, molds, and they produce less fruit of poorer quality. Many annuals tend to bolt when crowded, such as spinach, lettuce, radishes, and turnips.

While we used to think that weeds in the garden were not good, we have found in more recent studies that weeds can be our friends and helpers. As some herbalists say: weeds are plants we have not found a use for. Indeed many are coming into knowledge and usage in our very own garden, including in our biodynamics, our compost pile, and as edible food sources. Contrary to popular opinion, weeds do not necessarily sap nutrients and water from the soil, nor do they necessarily crowd out the plants. In reality, many weeds with long tap roots, such as burdock and dandelion, bring nutrients and trace minerals up to the surface of the soil and enhance the shallow rooted plants around them. Therefore, unless a "weed" is in direct competition with a plant, or has noxious chemicals or hormones being emitted from it, such as wormwood and deadly nightshade, we would reconsider pulling it and, in fact, would welcome it into our garden.

Some plants that are beneficial in ways I've mentioned are burdock, dandelion, and pigweed (also known in our area as lamb's-quarters) which is one of the best weeds for pumping nutrients from the subsoil and is a beneficial plant for potatoes, onions, and corn. It is also very edible, and we boil it or steam it in a similar manner to cooking spinach. Burdock root can be eaten. So can dandelion greens in salads. Stinging nettle, as a companion plant, or "weed companion" with tomatoes, will enhance the flavor, protect them from insect pests, and release nitrogen-enhancing hormones into the soil around the tomato plant. It is also an excellent plant for the compost pile, as it is a nitrogenous plant, like comfrey. They both will speed up the heating of your compost pile.

I would also urge you to rethink what "weed" means. I believe it was Ralph Waldo Emerson who said, "What is a weed? A weed is a plant whose virtues have not yet been discovered." James Russell Lowell said, "A weed is no more than a flower in disguise." A weed is simply an unloved flower, so we must learn to love them more. They grow wild with no help from us. No planting, fertilizing, or cultivating is necessary, and in the spring they can be worked back into the soil and they become valuable as mulch. They help to regulate the soil temperature, and the winter covering of weeds on the soil will help protect and increase the earthworm population. Weeds also help to hold nutrients in the soil. Without the natural ground cover of weeds many nutrients would be leached away or blown away by the wind. In other words, they are good for erosion contol when you are not using that space for your vegetables or flower garden. Weeds are also very important companion crops for your garden and for field plants.

The gardener should feel respect for himself and for his abilities as a gardener, for without this self-respect, he can feel no real respect for anything else: the Earth Mother, the plants, or the soil. Without self-respect, the gardener will do poor work, and his attitude alone will have a bad effect on the plants. Thinking in a positive manner toward the success of your garden will help to bring it about: your work will be better and more joyful, the plants will feel encouraged, and a positive attitude can only attract good spirits.

People coming into a garden area that has been consecrated should be made aware that they need to leave their negative attitudes, their egos, arrogance, and bad vibes on the compost pile or at the garden gate. The garden is a refuge where we raise our food and meditate on our relationship with the Earth Mother. It is a sacred place and should be celebrated as such.

Planning Your Garden

The work of raising a garden can be eased considerably by good planning. The health and well-being of your garden plants is affected, as well as the surrounding land, by the way your garden is planned and executed.

An ideal spot would be a gentle south slope (sun and drainage) just below a water source, with loamy soil, not shaded by trees. However, ideal spots are hard to come by and most of us are forced to compromise. The only thing that *must* be available is water. Everything else can be changed. Sandy soil can be improved by the addition of organic matter, shade (unless from rocks) can be removed, and the gardener can always walk a little farther.

Near the garden should be the compost heap. This is to avoid the time and energy spent on trucking or hauling finished compost to the garden.

Your watering system should be planned too, to do the job well without wasting valuable water. There are several watering systems a gardener can use, according to what is available and the type of climate he lives in.

The first of these methods is irrigation. This involves allowing large quantities of water to flow between the rows of vegetables and soak into the soil. This is a good method to use if plentiful water is available; it also takes a lot of work. Irrigating takes a lot of water, more than any other method, and the gardener has to put a lot of care into laying out his garden with carrying ditches so that the garden is watered evenly; it is very easy with irrigation to flood some parts of the garden and leave other parts dry. Despite its drawbacks, irrigation is the most commonly used watering system because once the system is set up it takes very little attention: letting the water in through a headgate or pump and periodic maintenance of the ditches. Care must also be taken to avoid erosion of the surrounding area because of the volume of water that must be used.

The second method for watering is sprinkling. This is a good system because it washes the plants while it waters them, and also cools them off. In very hot or dry climates sprinkling should be done in the evening or at night, both to conserve water and to avoid burning the plants. Water staying on the leaves of plants in hot sunlight will collect heat and burn leaves. The major drawbacks to sprinkling are: (1) expense (pipes, sprinklers, pump); (2) power (electricity for a pump or, as an alternative, a collection tank for gravity feed pressure); and (3) waste (much water, as much as 20 percent in hot, dry climates, will evaporate before the plants can use it). Another thing to remember is that sprinkling must be started before the ground begins to dry out in the spring.

The third system is drip irrigation. This is very similar to the first system, except that with drip irrigation the water is let into the ground very slowly and almost constantly. The ground is never allowed to become dry, as this will break the capillarity of the soil, meaning water can't get from the source to the plants without first flooding the garden. The chief advantage of drip irrigation is that very little water is wasted.

Subirrigation is very similar to drip irrigation except that no water at all runs over the surface of the ground. Perforated pipes are laid out *under* the ground, and water is sent into the system under low pressure, going up through the ground to the plants (capillary action). Again, great care must be taken not to allow the soil to dry out.

All four of these irrigation systems should be combined with a thick layer of mulch, for conservation of water and to prevent erosion. Mulch does many other things too, and will be discussed later.

Planning is required in deciding what to plant, as well as when to plant it and where in the garden.

First, consider your available space. If you have only a small garden area, you won't want to fill it with something which takes up a lot of space with a relatively low yield, such as corn, potatoes, or cabbages. One cabbage plant, yielding a five-pound cabbage, takes up a square yard. On the other hand, pole beans in the same space could yield up to twenty pounds. Check out how much space each plant needs for a good yield; a hint: roots take less space for a good yield, and many produce greens as well.

It is important not to overplant as this creates waste; plants and spirits resent this, seeing fruit they worked hard to produce being wasted. Care must be taken in planting heavy-yield plants such as tomatoes, zucchini, or things you would use little of, such as radishes. One tomato plant (medium-size tomato) can yield up to thirty pounds, one zucchini produces as much as twenty squashes.

A twenty-foot row of radishes will yield ten pounds, more than most families would use.

Where, and next to what, should be considered also. Cole family plants (cabbages, kale, broccoli, etc.) should be planted together, so that when you rotate the second year, they are all moved to an area where none of that family has grown for two years. Also, companion planting should be considered. This is planting combinations of plants which grow well together and repel each other's parasites: a good example of this is the Three Sisters, corn, squash, and beans, which have been grown together by Native people for many centuries.

Different areas and climates have differing companion combinations. Something universal, though, is that members of the onion family (onion, leek, garlic) will repel many but not all parasites.

Soil Preparations

Soil preparation, *before* you plant, is perhaps the most important part of your garden work. How the soil is prepared affects the garden throughout its growth, and also affects how well it resists disease and parasites.

For a first-year garden, the first step is to get rid of the wild plants (weeds). Many of these are edible (lamb's-quarters, wild mustard, tumbleweeds) or useful (yarrow, St. John's wort) but will crowd out your domestic, not so hardy vegetables. There are several ways of doing this: (1) spading: dig and pull, composting the weeds; (2) double-tilling: good in warm, long-season areas, but not practical for those with short summers—till in very early spring, wait one month so weeds will grow up in fresh soil, then till again to kill the weeds, plowing them into the soil; (3) slash-and-burn; the way many gardeners do it has both good and bad points—it kills weeds, seeds, and many insect eggs, but fails to kill roots of many perennial weeds. When combined with spading and caution, though, burning is a good method of getting rid of the weeds. However, we don't recommend it because of the adverse effect of the smoke on the atmosphere.

The next step in development of the garden is composting—adding organic matter to the soil. You shouldn't expect the soil to feed you unless you feed it. Composted, rotten horse or cow manure is ideal for a first-year garden. Lay it on about six inches thick and mix it well with the top foot of soil.

This must be done at least once a year, preferably twice: before planting and after harvest. I will speak more of compost later.

The other part of soil building is mulch, and this is a maintenance procedure carried on throughout the growing season.

Mulching means covering the ground between the plants with a layer of straw, dead leaves, or other organic matter. You can also use newspaper or black plastic, but these add nothing to the soil. A good cover of mulch helps retain moisture, retard weed growth, and keeps the soil from eroding or becoming packed hard. Mulch the garden well in the spring, after the ground is warmed up and the plants are well established and after all the first batch of weeds is pulled. Mulch will retard weed growth, but not stop it. Renew the mulch midway in the growing season, and again after the fall compost is dug in, to keep winter rain and snow from washing soil and nutrients away. Rake back the mulch before planting to allow the dark soil to collect heat.

Planting the Garden

We will start with early season, or frost-resistant vegetables. These can be planted as soon as the ground thaws in the early spring; many are also late season or fall planted crops.

1. Peas: Plant six inches apart and one inch deep; provide something for them to climb on. Peas are good for the soil; they fix nitrogen, an essential for plant growth.
2. Chard: Plant thinly and shallowly, then start thinning and eating as soon as they are four inches high; cook for greens or use raw for salad.
3. Spinach: Same as chard, except it grows faster.
4. Carrots: They should be sown a little more thickly, as the delicate seedlings have trouble breaking through the soil. Thin them when three inches high, then to six inches apart when first roots are edible.
5. Radishes: Sow one inch apart, one-quarter inch deep, thin to two inches when the fourth leaf appears, and use the greens.
6. The Cole family—cabbages, broccoli, kale, collards, and Brussels sprouts: You may plant these either as seeds in early spring (most are frost-resistant) or as plants. Space about twelve inches apart in rows two feet apart or more. Thin to three feet apart when four inches high.
7. Roots: Rutabagas, turnips, and beets are all frost-resistant. Sow thinly in rows or beds; thin to four inches apart when the third leaf appears, then eat the greens.
8. Tubers: Potatoes, sweet potatoes, and Jerusalem artichokes can all be planted in cold weather. Mulch over them immediately, as all these will grow right through mulch. Plant potatoes about eighteen inches apart; Jerusalem artichokes about two feet apart.

9. Onions: Plant seeds or sets as soon as ground is thawed, six inches apart.

A final note on cold weather planting: often seeds won't germinate until much later, sometimes waiting a full month until temperature and sunlight are right.

Starting Plants Early

Many plants which aren't frost-resistant must be started early indoors, especially in northern climates. Sow in flats (shallow wooden boxes) in rows three to four inches apart. Thin plants as soon as the third leaf appears. Be sure that the plants get enough sunlight: a south-facing window is sometimes enough.

Tomatoes, peppers, lettuce, the squash family, and the cole family may all be started indoors in this manner. Onions, leeks, and scallions, as well as many others, get a good start this way. These can all be transplanted outside as soon as frost danger is past. We start ours in February, giving a good margin in case we lose two or three flats.

Midseason Planting

Midseason crops are planted in late spring after the last frost and usually (except greens) harvested in fall.

1. Three Sisters: Corn, squash, and beans have been planted the same way for centuries. Hills, three feet apart, a foot high and wide, are planted with seeds of the sisters. You may want to soak the seeds overnight first so they get a head start of about four days. Well watered and cultivated, these three help keep each other healthy and pest free.

2. Tomatoes and peppers: Tomatoes should be planted three to four inches apart, then thinned to eighteen inches when five inches high. Peppers should be started early indoors in most areas of the United States and planted outdoors, a foot apart, when four inches high.

3. Melons: Plant in hills, three to four seeds to a hill. Make hills three feet apart, and thin to two strong plants per hill when four inches high.

4. Lettuce and other greens can be planted fairly thickly in rows a foot apart, or in beds. Thin when large enough to eat and all season long. Head lettuce is difficult to grow without pesticides; we prefer leaf lettuce.

5. Potatoes, peanuts, more beans, cucumbers, zucchini, pumpkins, and many other things can be planted in late spring.

Fall Planting

There are many crops that can be planted after the first harvest. These include many of the early spring crops: peas, chard, lettuce (hot summer not being good for growing lettuce), spinach, etc. This isn't a good time for roots because if they don't mature before the ground freezes, they go to seed in the spring. On the other hand, fall is a good time to plant garlic and onion sets, onion seed, and to replant some tubers like Jerusalem artichokes, for a crop the next fall. Garlic, if planted in spring, takes two full summers to come to maturity, but if planted in the fall, takes only one year.

This is also a good time to lay on a good thick layer of horse or cow manure, or finished compost, with a layer of mulch on top for the winter.

Maintenance After Planting

Proper care of the soil and plants ensures a bigger and better-quality harvest, and helps to control pest damage.

Water is the highest priority. Without sufficient water plants become stunted and much more vulnerable to insects.

Composting

Composting is the most important part of the gardener's work, for without good, rich compost, the soil will fail after one or two seasons, and the garden will fail before that, from pests or stunted plants.

We have seen many complex systems for making large quantities of finished compost, but we have found a very simple way that works well and fairly quickly. Start with a four-foot by six-foot wood structure that is a little more than four feet high. Make sure that the slats in your compost bin are about one-half inch apart to allow for aeration. Into this, place all the weeds you gathered clearing the garden. If you have nettles or comfrey growing nearby add these, as they will heat up the compost and speed decomposition. These are both nitrogenous plants, and nitrogen will make your compost hot. Coffee grounds or blood meal, which can be purchased at any nursery or plant supply place, also speeds up decomposition.

Use a foot or more of the weeds and other materials mentioned above as the first layer in your compost. If you don't have enough weeds you can supplement with straw, grass clippings, or pine needles. Cover this first layer with manure of some kind—either chicken, horse, or cow. Add a layer of wood ashes of any kind, then add another layer of vegetable matter, then more manure.

EARTH –
MANURE –
VEGETABLE
MATTER –
ASHES –
MANURE –
WEEDS –

Cover the whole pile with earth, seasoned manure from horse or cow, or rotten sawdust. Don't use fresh sawdust as it ties up the nitrogen in the soil, which is one of the main ingredients in making compost. Fresh sawdust can delay the decomposition of your compost by a year or more. Your completed pile should be about four feet high.

Cover it with a piece of plastic after saturating the pile with water. This keeps the water in and the chickens out. Anywhere in there except right on top can be your kitchen wastes, feathers from butchered chickens, or other miscellaneous organic matter. Let it cook (it really does: about 100 to 150 degrees) for about six weeks, then turn it and let it go another three weeks, after which it is ready to put on the garden.

More Maintenance

Weeding is also important. Some weeds crowd and shade plants when they are in direct competition with them. Weeds also attract insects. We nearly had our potatoes wiped out one year by a swarm of tiny beetle larvae that are a natural parasite on deadly nightshade, a close relative of the potato and a very common weed in the area.

Insect control is another priority. Much of this can be done by companion planting, soil maintenance, and weeding, but sometimes you have to go out and pick bugs off by hand.

There are other pests besides bugs; if you raise chickens, you'll have to fence the garden—or the chickens. Dogs likewise: we once had a whole zucchini and cucumber patch wiped out by one St. Bernard in a single trip across the garden.

Other pests are more difficult: moles, mice, and gophers. Rotating plastic garden daisies which create a vibration uncomfortable for burrowing rodents are some help. We have seldom been bothered by birds—on the contrary, birds in the garden are usually after bugs. If they are a problem for you, we suggest you get a good mouse-eating cat. She'll scare off the birds, and she'll keep the mice out of your stored harvest in the root cellar too.

Cultivating, or hoeing up earth around such plants as the coles, potatoes, and corn, is important too. This aerates the soil, softens it, and conserves water. An easier way is to lay on two or three layers of mulch through the season. This is especially important with potatoes: if young spuds are exposed to light they turn green and poisonous, like the leaves.

Mulch is a vital part of garden maintenance. Moisture is retained better, plants stay healthier, and erosion is stopped. Plants like broccoli, Swiss chard, and lettuce can be kept growing until the ground is frozen hard, by putting six to eight inches of straw or leaf mulch over the soil and plant.

The Harvest

Harvesting, and the care of your crops, is the last part of the year's gardening cycle.

Harvest plants like beets, turnips, and rutabagas when young and tender. Then place them in boxes of earth in your root cellar or back room. Onions and garlic should be allowed to dry in the sun for two to three days, then hung by the tops or stored in a dry place in mesh bags. Potatoes can be stored in sacks or bins in your root cellar. We also suggest freezing, canning, and drying for all of your garden vegetables. Waste nothing: feed excess and trimmings to your animals, or put them in the compost for the next year's garden.

Celebrate the harvest, and offer prayers of thanks for the bounty of Mother Earth, for if she is respected she feeds the spirit as well as the body.

Fruit

It is good to get fruit trees planted as soon as possible after moving to the country. It takes three to five years to get most varieties established. In the meantime, the trees will have to be protected from gnawing animals, both wild and domestic. They may even need extra watering.

Wild varieties of trees may be moved, too. That way you can be sure the tree is native to your area, but you will want to locate the trees in a place very similar to the old one. It is best not to transplant during the winter months when the sap is down because any damaged roots would cause the tree to bleed to death. Care should be used to prevent transplant shock. The trees should be handled gently, and great care taken not to damage the roots or expose them to harsh sunlight. The ball of earth around the root system should be kept intact if possible, and kept from drying out.

In planting, dig an adequate hole for the root structure of the tree. Put a cone or mound of earth back in the hole before setting the tree in. This step is to avoid air pockets which will prevent the tree from growing. Pour in water to be sure moisture will be near the roots when the tree is planted. Then set the tree on top of the cone and spread the roots evenly over it, as much in their natural position as possible. Fill in the dirt, a little at a time, making sure there are no clods or chunks to create air pockets. Water the tree again, soaking it thoroughly. Do not water it again for a week unless the weather is extremely hot and dry.

Berry shoots can be moved anytime after berries are harvested and before the leaves fall. They are extremely hardy and can withstand more handling and root breaking than most fruits. As long as the tap root isn't broken and the plants get enough water, the bushes will grow. Some kinds of berries will grow and take over your land. Find out what bushes do that so you can be selective. They are next to impossible to remove once established.

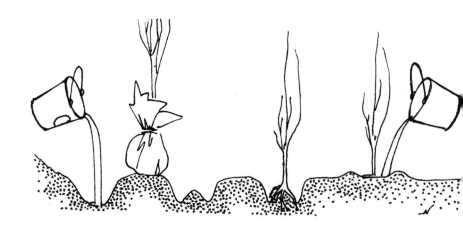

If you plan on extensive tree planting, or if you want to establish a little orchard, it is always best to learn all you can about the characteristics of different varieties of fruit. Seed nurseries will send you catalogs free which will describe them. If you still aren't sure, or if the words confuse you (like hybrid, F1, etc.), go to a garden center or other seedman, and ask him to help you understand the differences.

Like a garden, fruit trees require your care and love. At first they will need watering and a collar made from a can or milk carton to keep rabbits from chewing off the bark. When the trees grow older they will need pruning. Sometimes the branches will need support when they become loaded with fruit. Always, the trees need to feel that you respect them and their spirits.

Livestock

After you've had the satisfaction of planting and raising your own vegetables, you may want to go further and produce more of the things you need to survive. If you intend to eat meat you might want to consider raising animals for this. We feel it is irresponsible now to depend on hunting for meat as our wild four-legged brothers have already been too depleted. Home-grown meat is better for you than supermarket meat, as it hasn't been injected with toxic chemicals and hormones, and the animals have been raised with love and butchered with respect.

Rabbits

Putting aside the fact that a few people keep a rabbit or two for pets, let's consider raising rabbits for food. Rabbits are famous for being prolific, so they are a steady source of meat. Aside from that, there are other advantages to raising rabbits, as they require very little care and don't need much space to live in.

Rabbits can be raised in hutches (small screened-in box structures) or in wire mesh cages in a rabbit house. We started out with pens made of chicken wire with just the ground for a floor, but had to change the fence to small gauge wire, because even after they were pretty big the rabbits would squeeze right through the fence. As for the ground, they started digging out so fast that we soon had to install wooden floors in the pen, too. We also discovered that the wood had to be hard enough and thick enough so that the rabbits couldn't chew through it. At present our rabbits are housed in hanging all-mesh wire cages in a rabbit house.

Our rabbit cages are hung about three feet off the ground, and the floor area directly below the cages has a layer of sawdust which combines with the liquid and solid wastes from these four-leggeds, and eventually becomes the best manure compost our garden gets. Rabbit manure is the only manure than can be used directly on the soil without having to cure before use.

We had been told that the buck rabbits would fight if they were kept in the same area. They didn't. We were informed that the bucks and does wouldn't breed if they were kept in the same area all the time. They did. We were told that other adult rabbits would eat the newborn ones if they were all together. They didn't. There were little rabbits of all different sizes living with the full-grown ones. All these things had been explained to us by a man who had been raising rabbits for years. The only reason we can think of for all these rabbits doing so well is that we got them when they were young and let them grow up together.

Rabbits need feed at least twice a day, although they'll eat almost any time there's food. A grain or farm supply store usually carries bags of rabbit ration and salt spools. They also need a constant supply of clean water. Rabbits eat a lot, and they'll eat anything green. During the summer months, we pick up dandelions and alfalfa, wild oats, and quite a few other things, and feed them these as well as the ration. In the cold seasons, the produce man at a supermarket usually has lettuce trimmings and greens that anyone can get free for the asking.

If you don't want too many rabbits, it's a good idea to separate the bucks from the does. As for young ones, a doe rabbit generally always knows how to make a nest and take care of babies. As long as there's enough dry straw, she'll take care of the rest. Baby rabbits can squeeze through anything, so make sure their accommodations are designed to order. If a nest box, approximately twelve inches by fifteen inches by six inches deep, is provided for the doe a few days before she is due, and maintained half full of clean dry hay or straw, the babies will remain warm and content in the enclosure until old enough to hop out on their own.

When you have rabbits, one thing is inevitable: they'll get out. When domestic rabbits are out, you won't be the only one trying to catch them. Owls, hawks, stray dogs, coyotes, and quite a few other animals like to eat rabbits, so keep a close watch on your hutch.

Chickens

Chickens provide a good supply of meat and eggs if they're properly cared for.

The most economical way to raise them is to start with baby chicks, since they don't cost much. Your first concern should be building a chicken coop that is insulated well enough to protect the chicks from rain, wind, and cold weather. It should also be built well enough to protect chickens from rats, skunks, and various other predators. It should have at least one window. Chickens don't need a wooden floor, but the ground should be covered with straw. Your coop should have enough space so they don't get crowded, a minimum of two square feet per chicken.

While they're young, chicks can be kept warm at night and during cold weather by two two-hundred-watt lamps about a foot off the floor. They should be provided with a constant supply of clean water, and fed an adequate amount of chick scratch once each morning and evening.

As they grow larger and get their heavy feathers, the food can be changed to your own organic mix of corn, wheat, barley, soy beans, oats, and oyster shell, and the heat source can be reduced to one two-hundred-watt bulb raised higher off the ground. Not long after this, chickens will show a tendency to sit (roost) on something higher above the ground. A roost can be built by constructing a rectangular framework of one-inch slats about six inches apart and eighteen inches above the floor.

About this time, your chickens can be let outside in the morning to scavenge. When it gets dark they'll come back inside to roost. It is inevitable that you'll lose some chickens to predators, injury, or disease. Do not hesitate to destroy a hurt or sick bird. It will release it from suffering, and it will protect the rest of the flock from the same disease. Because of possible losses, it's a good idea to start with about 10 percent more chickens than you expect to end up with.

As far as chicken diseases go, there are more of them than can be mentioned in this book. But don't worry! Chicken diseases are regional and each area usually is affected by only two or three. Also, most of the diseases are very rare. The best source of information on diseases in your area is your local feed-grain farm supply store, not a veterinarian.

As your chickens get older, you'll be able to see very definitely which are roosters and which are hens. You don't need a lot of roosters, but you should keep at least one for each ten hens if you want fertile eggs. Of course this means the hens will need nests about a foot square and a foot off the ground. Wooden nest boxes with open fronts will work well so you don't need to crawl around on the floor to look for eggs. The reason you won't want to do this is because the floor will be covered with chicken manure, but most of it should accumulate under the roost.

After the manure builds up, it can be removed with a shovel and used as compost (fertilizer). It should be cleaned out every time it builds up to a few inches deep. It's good for your garden since it's a natural source of nitrogen.

After the chickens reach the adult stage, you need only feed them twice a day and collect eggs in the evenings. If you decide you need more chickens, just let a hen or two keep all her eggs. She'll do all the rest until the chicks hatch, then you start all over with the lights, chick scratch, and such.

After a certain age, chickens will eat almost anything that grows from the Earth Mother. It is from the energy of the Earth Mother that they grow and produce, the same as you. Just take care of a few things for them and the Earth Mother will take care of them and you as well.

Care of a Cow

Have you ever thought about having a cow? One cow can give a couple of gallons of milk a day. What does that mean? Well, even figuring at $1.80 a gallon, that's $3.60 a day or almost $1,100 a year, after subtracting the two months when she has her calf. If she has a heifer calf, you've got another potential milk cow. If it's a bull calf, you've got your own meat supply.

When a cow has a calf, milk production will increase to about four gallons a day. That's enough so you can have one and a half to two gallons after the calf gets its share. If that's more milk than you can use, you can make cheese, cottage cheese, yogurt, butter, buttermilk, and whipped cream from it. If you're lucky like us and have an ice cream churn, you can make superior ice cream.

If you use the calf for meat, this can account for 24 to 40 percent of your total food bill—and that's all from one cow.

A healthy cow might cost between $600 and $800. Then she'll need a shelter, which shouldn't cost more than $100 if you use inexpensive materials. Ours didn't cost anything.

You'll need straw for the floor of her barn, about $25 worth per year. It will take about two acres of pasture. You will probably need oats (never barley) and sometimes a milk-producing supplement, but that shouldn't cost over $300 a year. You'll also need about two tons of alfalfa hay at $50 to $75 per ton.

There may be some veterinary bills, up to $75 to $100 a year, but a very reasonable sum to insure the health of the cow. It's a good thing to get your cow from someone you know, so you'll know you're getting a healthy cow to begin with. If you don't know anyone in the business, cows do sell very cheaply at auction yards, but be cautious. There is bound to be a reason why they're being sold. Have her checked by a vet as soon as you have her home.

With a cow, you must be willing to take the time she requires. She needs two milkings and two feedings a day—twelve hours

A former Bear Tribe Holstein cow, Snow, and her calf Harry

apart is ideal. A six-inch plug of hay and a quart and a half of oats or grain supplement will hold her through each milking.

You will need a few simple pieces of equipment. One is a stainless steel milk bucket, to be thoroughly cleaned with dairy detergent, then scalded after each use. Also, cheesecloth for straining the milk. You'll also need a rope halter and a lead rope and a watering trough and feed box. These things shouldn't cost over $50.

A cow project might cost up to $1,600 to get started, but it will produce $1,100 per year in milk, plus 24 to 40 percent of your food bill if your cow has a bull calf.

Preserving Food

In this day and age, we have several choices open to us for food preservation. Almost any of these is preferable to buying manufactured food at a supermarket at inflated prices. If you have a garden of your own, have fruit trees, or raise your meat, you will be able to feed your family much better for much less money than city people can. If you don't raise all your own food, there are other ways of getting quantities of it, such as gleaning, buying directly from the grower, and trading. You must be willing to invest your time, and learn the best methods for certain foods to preserve their flavor and quality and keep them safe for consumption.

It is possible to preserve foods by canning, freezing, drying, smoking, and root-cellar storage.

Freezing

Today, people are discovering that freezing food, both raw and cooked, is easier than canning and preserves nutrients, color, texture, and flavor better. It makes it possible to take advantage of quantity buying when foods are in season, or when special sales are available. It is possible to freeze leftovers for use at another time or to prepare in advance for holiday and company meals. Wise use can make it possible for any family to eat better on less money and conserve the time of the people for other activities.

Some fruits and vegetables should be blanched (steamed quickly or boiled for two or three minutes, then immersed in cold water) before freezing. It is best to check in the freezer manual for the correct amount of time to blanch each type of food.

Meat should be ready to use before being wrapped. It is very difficult to do anything with a frozen solid piece of meat. Be sure to wrap it twice to prevent freezer burn. Take care to rotate the food in the freezer every month or two. Put dates on your labels.

There is a disadvantage to freezing. If the electricity is out for any length of time, you're out of luck.

Canning

There are different methods of canning different foods: cold packing, pressure canning, and open kettle canning. Be sure to follow the correct directions, since the bacteria causing botulism may now be present in your soil, even if they weren't in the past. Botulism can be carried from place to place and infect the soil, and if your canned food contains this bacterium, it will grow in the presence of moisture to become very poisonous, often deadly. Many times in the past, people have eaten vegetables or meat improperly processed and not become ill because the soil was not infected, *but you cannot be sure.*

Most agricultural extension services have good free books on canning. Most cookbooks have canning sections. You can also buy the *Ball Blue Book* or the Kerr Company canning book. These are reputable firms. Follow the instructions exactly. Have the book open as you can the food.

Before starting any canning process, inspect your jars carefully and discard any with even a tiny nick. Wash and rinse them thoroughly. Some canning methods require you to sterilize the jars. This is done by boiling them in a pan, with some water in the pan and in each jar, for twenty minutes. The rings and seals should also be sterilized. Before you begin, read the specific instructions for what you are canning, and be sure you have everything you need and that it is in good condition.

After each batch has been canned, lift it out of the canner and put it where it can stay undisturbed while it cools. There should be good air space around each jar so it can cool evenly and seal

properly. Then test the seals. The cooling of the jar causes a vacuum to form inside and pull the "dome" lid down. If this does not happen, the jar hasn't sealed, and most likely won't if the jar has cooled off. You'll have to either eat the food right away, or can it again with a new seal. Under no circumstances should you try to use a seal a second time.

When you get ready to use your canned foods, you will be able to tell that they have a good seal by inspecting them, pushing on the lid, or hitting it with metal. If you hear a hollow thump, throw it out. If you are in doubt, throw it out. Botulism poisoning is serious, sometimes fatal.

The basic steps in canning are these: choose good, firm fruit or vegetables, unless you are trying to save a crop; wash, cut, peel, pit, whatever is appropriate; cut out any bad spots; pack the fruit or vegetables into the jars no higher than one-half inch from the top; add water or syrup; wipe the rims of the jars clean, then put the seals and rings on tight. Next you process the jars, either under pressure or in a canning kettle, according to complete instructions.

Drying

We are fairly experienced at home drying and have run the gamut of successes and failures. We know what works for us, and wish to share it here.

From our point of view, drying is the most practical way of preserving food. Almost any fruit, vegetable, meat, or grain can be dried. We have heard of local Indians drying duck eggs.

The main thing to remember in *any* method of storage is the list of things that affect the overall quality of food—and they are *moisture, light, pests,* and *temperature.*

We don't sulfur anything. Some say that sulfuring saves the vitamin C in fruit (but destroys the B-complex). It does preserve the color. We're willing to lose the color to preserve the natural taste. People have been drying things for at least five thousand years without sulfur.

Basically, drying is the removal of *moisture,* which is the growth medium for bacteria, fungi, and molds. Sufficiently dried foods keep very well. They eventually deteriorate, but so do foods preserved by any other means.

We have found that it takes a real group effort to prepare large quantities of fruit or vegetables for drying. Removal of pits and cores requires a good sense of humor, endurance, and a willingness to get sticky. Unblemished fruit and vegetables dry best, but we've dried "culls" (seconds) with success after cutting the blemishes out. If you suspect pesticides have been used, wash whatever you want to dry.

We dry most things in the sun on cardboard flats. We spread the fruit or vegetables out in a single layer, making sure the pieces don't touch (that causes rot), turn it sometimes for even drying, and let the sun do the work. This method works if there are no flies (*pests*), you don't have chickens, and your area doesn't get much rain or heavy dew (*moisture*). Cheesecloth held down with clothespins takes care of the fly problem. A fence, either around the fruit or around the chickens, will take care of the pecking and other poultry problems. And a team of fast people can bring the fruit in the house every night or if it rains.

We now have good success at drying foods using a simple solar dryer. The dryer is constructed like a cabinet on stilts, with a solar panel sloping down from the bottom of the cabinet to the ground on the southern exposure.

A solar panel is fairly easy to build. Take a piece of corrugated tin roofing material smaller than four feet by eight feet and build a shallow box to hold it, say about four inches deep and eight feet long by four feet wide (a piece of plywood works well as a back for this box). Name one of the four-foot by four-inch sides the bottom end, and the other the top end. There must be screened vents in the bottom and top ends. The area of these openings should be in a ration of three (bottom) to six (top). Paint the inside of the box flat black. You can buy a special paint for solar absorbence which does absorb sunlight better than regular paint, but the panel will work without a special paint. Paint the roofing material with the same flat-black paint and nail it into the box. Cover the entire box with a piece of plate glass and seal it with silicon sealant. You can use clear plastic, but this will not work as well as glass.

Let's call the south side of the cabinet the front and the north the back. The front of the cabinet must be at least four feet wide at the bottom to accommodate the top of the solar panel making entry into the bottom of the cabinet. The opening in the cabinet should be no bigger than is necessary to allow the top end of your solar panel to make entrance, and can be sealed with duct tape. We have the entire back of this cabinet as a door that can be opened fully. The inside of the cabinet has been lined with shelf guides about two inches apart and we have built racks to slide onto these guides out of braced one-by-ones covered with plastic screening (the metal used in most screening can release toxic substances). At the top-back of the cabinet there is another screened opening that is three times the area at the bottom end of the solar panel (so for every

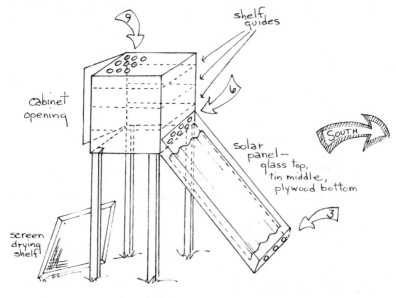

Solar Dryer Sketch

three square inches of opening at the bottom end of the panel you have six square inches open at the top end of the panel, and nine square inches open at the top-back of the cabinet for proper flow of heated air through the dryer).

The solar panel works best if it is facing due south and is at an angle that is perpendicular to the noonday sun.

We know of people who make and use other kinds of dryers that utilize electricity for the drying procedure. If you are interested in making one of these dryers, consult the books available on the subject. The optimum drying temperature is 120 degrees Fahrenheit.

Most fruits dry easily by the methods already described. Some notable exceptions are watermelon and nonraisin grapes. We have dried strawberries and other berries by sewing them together in garlands and hanging them by both ends. We know that Pueblo Indians dry melons by quartering them and peeling them, then hanging them on a line in the sun. We haven't tried it yet.

Most fruits are quite edible in dry form if you have good teeth, but they can all be reconstituted by soaking several hours in water or by boiling, with or without sweetener.

In the vegetable department, we've dried zucchini, celery, cut corn, onions, cabbage, carrots, peppers, and string beans. String beans must be dried slowly in the shade. We strung them on thread and decorated our office with them for almost a month. These are called Leather Britches beans, and you cook them several hours with a hambone if you have one. Unless you're drying a stringless variety, it is wise to string them before drying.

Meats and fishes are easily dried. Jerky is made by cutting the meat in thin strips and sewing it together. The whole string can be boiled rapidly for three minutes in very salty water (10 percent solution, one that floats an egg) and hung to dry for three to ten days, depending on the moisture in the air. Meat strips can also be put in a pan with salt packed between the layers for a day before you string them. Small fish filets can be salted well and hung until dry. Fish and meat can also be smoked, but we haven't tried it yet.

The *storage* of dried foods is just as important as the drying. Be sure all the food is completely dry. The drier it is, the longer it will keep. Package it in small plastic bags and seal them tightly with twister seals. The reason for the small batches is that if spoilage *does* begin, it will stay within the one bag. The *moisture* will not spread easily to others. We freeze each bag for at least forty-eight hours to kill any bugs—bacteria, larvae, or whatever. Then we put the little bags in airtight containers, as the lack of *oxygen* retards the growth of some bacteria. Then we store the whole works in a fairly dark, cool place.

One lifesaver has been rotating the food every two months or so. This gives you a better idea of how fast you're using certain foods and what you have left. You can discard any bags that might have spoiled. It is also an opportunity to see whether or not you need mousetraps in your storage area. It is a good idea to have a reminder that our enemies are *moisture, light, heat,* and *pests.* Although light, heat, and oxygen helped us to dry the foods to begin with, they do nothing to improve the flavors and nutrition of the food once it is dry.

Smoking

Smoking meat and fish is a slow process for removing the moisture which causes spoilage and for permeating it with smoke, which acts as a natural preservative. A smoldering fire is built of hardwood, and a low temperature (never over 90 degrees Fahrenheit) is maintained in the smoke chamber.

Remember that it takes time, not heat, to dry the meat.

Meat is cleaned and prepared by cutting it in slices and hanging it in an enclosure where smoke can reach all surfaces. Uneven

smoking will not preserve the meat. Fish may be smoked whole if they are not too large, but they must be opened out so that smoke reaches every inside and outside surface. No piece of fish or meat should be touching anything.

The fire should be made with hardwood, such as hickory or alder. Soft woods are not suitable. A smoke tunnel is needed to conduct the smoke, but not the heat, from the fire to the smoking chamber. It is sometimes best to install a simple baffle to distribute the smoke evenly in the smoke chamber.

Cool smoking will preserve the meat. If the meat becomes too hot, it will cook, and then it must be frozen, canned, or eaten immediately.

Northwest Native people have used cool smoking to preserve their salmon and other meat for many centuries, and many of them have impressive smokehouses just for that purpose.

Root Cellars

A root cellar is very important when you raise your own vegetables and fruits. It functions in several ways. It is used to store your tuberous vegetables, fresh and canned food, and, in some cases, serves as a storm cellar. It is comparatively simple to construct, although it takes a lot of hard work with a shovel.

First you dig a pit about the size of an average room in a house, if this will be adequate for your needs, with a slightly sloping floor for drainage. The walls can be lined with rock and mortar or other materials, if you choose, or if you are uncertain of the lasting value of the walls otherwise. Rock is a good material to use in a root cellar because it gives the desired coolness.

Be sure there is adequate drainage from your root cellar. Stagnant water is not something you want in with your food.

The pit should be covered, except for the entrance, with a cover that will support the weight of the earth that will cover it to give it its insulated qualities. An insulated door is necessary, and a ladder or steps. When you have shelves for canned goods, and bins lined with good wheat straw, your cellar is finished.

The purpose of the cellar is to preserve your food. Milk and eggs can be set there as well as potatoes, rutabagas, carrots, cabbage, beets, onions, pumpkins, squash, and melons. Winter apples do extremely well there. Be sure to pack everything but potatoes and carrots in straw. The potatoes and carrots should be packed in boxes of earth. Be careful to pack vegetables well so they do not touch each other, because they will rot where they touch if they are left for long enough. During summer months your root cellar can preserve many vegetables and fruits you would otherwise have to refrigerate.

It is very important to check your stored foods every few weeks to remove any that might be bad. Ultimately, this effort will reduce spoilage.

Storing for Survival

It is our belief that mainly those people living on the land in groups in harmony with each other and the Earth Mother will survive the coming cleansing of the earth. For these groups to survive, they must be prepared. That means that they must have stored enough supplies to sustain the group for a period of three or more years.

What will you need to survive? First of all, water. If you have chosen your land well, you will have a good natural water supply that will flow without interruption. A spring or well is the best alternative. If you get your water from a stream it might be cut off or become unsafe during certain periods of the cleansing of the earth. To make sure you'll have some water if such periods arise you should fill some glass or plastic containers with fresh water, store in a safe place, and check every few months for leaks and freshness. Figure on a minimum of one-half gallon of water per person per day for drinking. To use water that is unsafe, purify it by boiling for one to three minutes, then pour it from one container to another several times to get some air and flavor back in. You may also purify it by adding any bleach that has hypochlorite as its only active ingredient (eight drops to a gallon of clear water, sixteen if the water is cloudy), letting the water sit for half an hour and checking that the chlorine smell is still there. If it isn't, add another dose of the bleach and let stand for another fifteen minutes. You may also use three percent tincture of iodine. Add twelve drops to a gallon of clear water, and twice that to cloudy. Or you can use water purification tablets if you have them. These methods are useful when the water is unsafe because of bacteria or other organisms. They will not help with chemical pollution or radioactivity.

Alternatively, you can use granular activated charcoal (GAC). It can be used by pouring water through the GAC in a coffee Melitta with a coffee filter.

Next you should have on hand a large supply of any herbal or prescription medication needed by members of your group: contraceptives, heart pills, allergy pills, insulin, etc. Then, of course, you'll need food, and seeds, canning and drying equipment, fishing and hunting gear. Having a varied diet is very essential to keeping your balance, so we really urge any of you who think you can live completely off the land to rethink your plan. While you can get your meat through hunting, and forage for wild greens, berries, herbs, and fruits, we believe that this can be irresponsible as it puts too much strain on the Mother Earth at this time. If you have a good supply of seeds, you can grow your own vegetables, then can or dry them for the fall, winter, and spring when you can't get them fresh. Besides canning equipment (remember to have three or four times the number of lids, as jars and rings) you'll need sugar or honey for canning fruits and jams, salt for vegetables, and vinegar, dill, and spices for pickling.

Because growing a garden may be difficult or impossible for a year or two, we suggest that you have canned foods and dried ones on hand. For a family of five you'll need, on the average, two cans of soups per day, two of vegetable, one meat, and two fruit, plus five cans of juice per week. In addition, for a year you'll need at least twelve three-pound cans of shortening, six cans of baking powder, and eight gallons of bleach for water and other purification.

Besides your fruits, juices, and vegetables, you'll also need some staples. With a mixed diet, an adult will use three hundred pounds of wheat per year, or one hundred pounds of flour. Wheat is cheaper to get and easier to store than flour. Make sure to get a hand-powered grinder with a stone buhr to grind the wheat. Each adult will also need eighty pounds of powdered milk, one hundred and fifty pounds of dried beans and peas (including soybeans, your best nonmeat source of protein), sixty pounds of honey, and fifty pounds of peanut butter per year. In addition to the above, store any items that you're used to having in your diet: for instance, coffee, tea, herbs for tea, oats, rice, barley, nuts, hard candies, salt, pepper, spices, vinegar, oil, desserts, cornmeal, potatoes, syrup, molasses. To figure out how much you need to store, mark boxes or jars and see how much you use over a two-week period, and multiply by twenty-six for a year's supply. Store things that will keep well and store them in moisture-, mouse-, and insect-proof containers.

What hunting and fishing gear you'll need depends on what you are used to and can use. Unless you think you want to be vegetarian (which may not be practical in a period when vegetables may not grow well) you should know how to use something. A .22 is a good all-around rifle, but you have to be a good shot to get small game with it. Shotguns are good for that. Get the right ammunition for the guns you have, and get plenty of it. For fishing get plenty of line, an assortment of hooks, flies, sinkers, and a float. You can make your own pole, and later, your own flies. In case you hit a period where no game is available to you we suggest having a supply of jerky, dried fish, and canned meat and fish on hand.

You should also have in storage (or in use) tools that you are likely to need. These should include a good case skinning knife, a sharpening stone, a double-bit axe, a saw, shovel, hammer, screwdrivers, nails, screws, hoe, spade, pliers, pots, pans, plates, bowls, silverware, longhandled fork, towels, sheets, matches, several canvas tarps or large pieces of heavy plastic, a fire grill, canteens, washboard, rope, pails, can openers, and other utensils for cooking and eating. And you should stock up on sanitary and personal items: soaps of all kinds, disinfectants, cleaning solutions, toilet paper, sufficient bedding for everyone, personal clothes, sweaters, heavy jackets and rain ponchos, sewing equipment, craft supplies, good hiking or woodsman boots, boots or overshoes for winter, work gloves, tooth equipment (include dental floss), sanitary napkins, extra underwear, alcohol, ammonia, aspirin, bandages, Band-Aids, cotton, eardrops, Epsom salts, Paregoric, safety pins, shampoo, thermometers, tweezers, antihistamine, linament, calamine lotion, Vaseline, snakebite kits, insect repellent, and vitamins. You'll probably also want reading and writing material, cards, and other games.

You'll also need to store different fuels to combat the present fuel shortages, and the worse ones that we'll face in the future. Gasoline is a good fuel that can not only power your car but also generators and various other things. It can be stored in the metal gasoline cans made specifically for that purpose, or in metal drums. For reasons of both safety and security it is probably best to bury the drums, and not let people see what you are doing. Unleaded gasoline can also be used to fuel Coleman stoves and lanterns. We don't feel that either natural or propane gas will be available for use for an indefinite period, nor do we recommend storing them. Other than gasoline, the only other fuel we feel will be relevant is wood (or possibly coal if you're in an area where it is available). Wood is a good fuel for both heating and cooking, and it is easily available in most areas. We think that you'll be safe if you just have a year's supply ready in advance. In any case, you should always get in your winter's supply before it gets too wet and cold to do so. Four to eight cords of wood should be enough for the heating and cooking needs of a four-room cabin, depending on the area where the cabin is located. For additional light needs, you should have a good supply of candles, flashlights, batteries, kerosene lanterns, and kerosene.

We know that we've suggested storing a substantial amount of goods of all kinds and that it will be costly to do so. However, we can't think of any safer investment you can make. While we are geared to having small groups together on the land, we feel that you should start storing these supplies wherever you are and whatever your family structure. We do urge city dwellers to at least think of places in the country where they might be able to store some of their supplies. We think you should start gathering your storage supplies now. While we can't put a date on when we think this system will destroy itself completely, we don't think there is much time left. And it's better to have your survival supplies ready ten years too early than an hour too late.

Making Meat

For those who like to eat meat, hunting is an essential skill. There may be times when vegetarians will have to eat meat or starve, so everyone should know how to hunt if they have to. Before beginning, always pray to the guardian spirit of the animal you seek. Explain that you have need of one of its sons or daughters to continue your life, and that you, too, will someday feed the Earth Mother. When you make a kill, always thank the animal for giving its life and pray for its spirit to go quickly to the Great Spirit.

When we have to hunt in hot weather we catch fish and hunt small animals like ground squirrels, woodchucks, etc. (although care must be taken with small, furry animals during the summer because of rabies and because cases of the plague have been reported in the Southwest and West). We hunt big game in the fall and winter. In cold climates, if you hunt in November you can freeze your meat and it will keep outside in a shed all winter. Do cut the meat before it freezes.

In hunting, especially still hunting, patience is important. If you find a water hole where game comes to water you may have to come back and sit more than one evening to get meat. In deer country if you put out salt near one of their runways you can get them coming there regularly. If you make a kill, clean up all of the blood and cover it over so as not to scare off other game. Late afternoon or early evening is the best time to hunt deer and rabbit. In stalking game, try to blend into the surrounding country as much as possible. Placing grass on your hat and binding brush to your arms will change your appearance enough to enable you to get close to game. Wear brown, grey, greens, black, or levi blue, no white or bright colors. The Indian bowman knew he had to get close in order to get meat with his bow and arrow. Sometimes it might have taken half a day of stalking, but time wasn't the important factor. Food was. So if it takes all day to get meat, fine. At the same time, you're enjoying the countryside.

A 45- or 50-pound bow with blade head hunting arrows is good for the bowman. And you can learn how to shape your arrowheads from obsidian or flint using a deer antler or nail to flake them off, and then, by feathering your own shafts, you are one step closer to self-reliance.

If you want to use guns, two of the best are the 20-gauge over-under, or the 410-gauge .22 over-under. A .22 rifle is a good all around gun. A .22 repeater long rifle with hollow-point shells is best. Shotguns are good, and they'll keep you in small game like ducks, grouse, and rabbits. Buy good ammunition.

Get yourself a good case skinning knife. You don't need a big machete on your hip if you get a good knife. Keep it sharp, and know how to use it.

To skin rabbits, squirrels, and other small game, cut around the back legs by the feet, and then cut down the inside of the legs to the rectum. It's best to put the point of the knife under the skin and cut. Then work the skin free from the body using both your fingers and knife. Pull the skin over the body toward the front legs. Cut carefully around the legs, cutting the skin free at the wrist of the paw. Take your time around the ears and eyes if you want to save the whole hide. On rabbits you can just cut the skin off at the neck. Use wire coat hangers bent into shape to stretch the pelts. Now, to prepare the carcass of small game for cooking, cut off the feet and the head, then cut into the stomach and draw out the entrails. You can then reach up into the rib cage and draw out the heart and liver, both of which make good eating. Wash the meat in water. If it's bloody, let it sit overnight in cold water.

In skinning deer and other big animals, first cut the throat to bleed the meat. Cut the skin around the back legs, then cut down the inside of the legs to the rectum, cut around the rectum, then cut down the belly between the front legs to the throat. Cut around the front legs and then work the hide off. If you can, hang the animal from a tree by the hind legs, as it's easier to skin. Otherwise, skin it out by using your hands to pull, and cut with your knife where necessary. Keep the carcass on the skin if skinning on the ground. Cut through the belly and remove the entrails. Cut into the chest cavity and remove lungs, heart, and liver. Cook up the heart and liver the first night. Give the lungs to your pets. Wiggle the legs and you can see where to cut at the joints. Cut through the meat around the backbone, then cut the ribs loose by first splitting the breast plate with either a heavy knife or a hatchet, and then cut the ribs away from the backbone. Cut chops and steaks from the legs and back. The rest of the meat is good for roasting, stew meat, or soup bones. Remember to use all of the meat. Don't waste the gifts that the four-leggeds have given to you.

Fishing

Hook and line is probably the most often used method of fishing. You should have the fishing equipment you are used to, but if you don't, you can improvise. The point is to catch food, not the sport of game fishing. A variety of hooks will equip you for different kinds of fish, depending on where you plan to fish. A pole can be made of a switch from a large bush or from a branch. All it does is enable you to get your baited hook to the fish.

Suitable bait is anything that looks good to a fish. It can be a piece of cheese, corn, worms, or a fly that looks juicy. Learn where the fish hang out (on the bottom, in the shady eddies, etc.). Do not think you can't catch fish without the usual equipment. A little imagination and prayer go a long way.

Nets can be used for catching fish, either by scooping them out of the water when they run heavy, or by securing a net in a body of water where fish are likely to be.

Don't take the lives of fish unless you need to. Be sure you understand the law in your state with regard to fishing. In some places the use of nets is illegal, and the catch limit will vary according to what kind of fish you're after. Remember to make your prayers, the same as you would when you take any other animal or plant life.

Wild Plants

While we feel that relying solely on wild plants is irresponsible at this time because they have been reduced dangerously in numbers by human carelessness, we do feel they can be used sparingly to supplement one's diet.

When we need to pick an herb or plant we always approach it with humility and respect. We tell the herbs why we need them and how we plan to use them. We never pick the first of any herb or other wild food that we see. Rather, we make an offering of tobacco, cornmeal, or of a special prayer. We never take from the Earth Mother and our fellow creatures without giving also.

We always harvest the plants quickly but carefully, so as not to prolong the trauma of picking. While harvesting, we continually give thanks in our hearts. We never "clear cut" a plant patch. It is important to leave enough plants growing so that they can replace themselves and multiply, assuring plentiful wild plants for this generation and all generations to come.

When picking wild plants it is always wise to be cautious. Some poisonous plants closely resemble edible ones. Following are some safety hints on edible plants:

1. There is no general reliable test for poisonous plants, such as milky juice being present or absent. For instance, the dandelion has milky juice and is edible, whereas some of the most poisonous plants do not have it.

2. Wild animals eat various poisonous plants. However, they have a different digestive system and these same plants may poison humans.

3. Livestock usually avoid toxic plants if others are available, but in the spring and when they are hungry they will graze on poisonous plants, sometimes with fatal results.

4. Some plants are poisonous when they are wilted, such as chokecherry twigs and some grasses. Therefore, use fresh plants.

149

5. The toxic property may be concentrated or even confined to one part of the plant, such as the elderberry where all parts are poisonous with the exception of the *ripe* purple-black berries.

6. In some cases, cooking tends to destroy the poison in the plant, but this doesn't hold true in all cases.

7. Don't use any wild plants that look like wild carrot or parsley unless you're absolutely sure of your species. It may be poison hemlock.

8. Don't eat white or red-colored berries without being absolutely sure of the plant. Use caution on blue or black berries; even some of them are poisonous.

9. It is best to avoid *all* mushrooms and toadstools (except the ones that you buy at the store) as even experts have been fooled as to which ones are poisonous and which are edible. Caution: The edibility test is not reliable on mushrooms as some species do not show symptoms of poisoning for up to three days. A pea-size portion of some mushrooms can kill you. It only takes one mistake.

10. Don't eat any plants from soil that is known to contain selenium or from soil where plant "indicators" of selenium grow. Some common plants that indicate selenium are milk vetch (locoweed), wild asters, golden weed, and saltbush (greasewood).

11. Some plants such as lamb's-quarters absorb toxic levels of nitrates from commercial fertilizers. Avoid these plants in commercially fertilized areas.

12. Avoid plants close to main roadsides, as many times they are sprayed with toxic weed control chemicals as well as the exhaust of cars.

13. Be sure you know the plant in its very young stages as well as other stages of growth.

14. A wild plant is not necessarily edible just because it looks somewhat like a well-known species.

15. Always use caution in trying any type of unknown plant even if you think you're sure; some poisonous effects are cumulative.

16. Many plants are toxic if they are moldy. Use fresh plants.

17. The fungus ergot is poisonous and will affect several types of grain. Avoid grain that has turned a dark color and is several times the size of other individual grains.

18. Learn the common poisonous plants of the area, particularly those that may be mistaken for edible plants.

19. Build your recognition list of edible plants with great care so that you are familiar with them at all stages of growth. It is better to be too cautious than to end up in the hospital or cemetery.

20. Don't gorge yourself on unfamiliar food until your system becomes used to it.

21. Whenever possible, eat the plants raw, since prolonged boiling tends to get rid of vitamins and enzymes very quickly.

22. When boiling wild plants it is wise to use several changes of water. Throw away the first one as it may be too bitter.

23. Don't eat wild plants when you know radiation levels are high in the area.

There are many varieties of plants you can eat safely. Following are some common ones we like which grow in most areas of the country. The list just gives you a few ideas of the many plants that are edible. If you want to know more, consult the many good books now available on the subject.

Acorns. The Indians are very fond of these nuts. We gather them in the fall as they drop from the trees. If left on the ground they will get wormy. We shell them and then leach out the bitterness by pouring hot water over them and draining them repeatedly. Then we grind them and use them as flour mixed with other meal, or we add them to beans and soups.

Burdock. Young tender shoots can be peeled and eaten raw or fried in butter or oil. They can also be mashed and made into cakes and fried in butter.

Cattails. Young shoots can be cleaned and eaten raw like celery, or they can be steamed with other vegetables. The "sausage" top can also be steamed and eaten like corn on the cob.

Dandelion. Young leaves can be used in a salad, or older leaves can be boiled in two changes of water to remove the bitterness for a green vegetable similar to spinach or beet tops. These greens have a large amount of vitamin A.

Lamb's-quarters. These make a fine summer potherb. They grow almost anywhere. They should be boiled in two changes of water, which does away with any bad taste they may have picked up.

Milkweed. The young shoots of milkweed also may be boiled, although older stems are too acid and milky for use. Young pods are excellent when cooked.

Mustard. These greens are excellent cooked. They will aid your digestion. The roots can be ground as a garnish for meat.

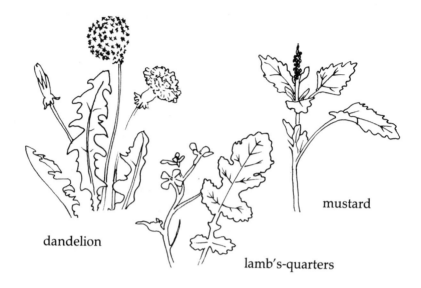

dandelion

mustard

lamb's-quarters

Pine nuts. The cone of the piñon pine yields a small nut inside a thin shell. They are harvested by Indian people in Nevada, California, New Mexico, and other places. They are usually roasted and eaten hot, although they can be eaten raw or in a soup.

Wild fruit and berries. Many wild berries are edible. Many are eaten raw. Many, along with other wild fruits, are good dried or even canned for later use.

Wild oats. This grain is roasted or singed over a fire to get rid of the sharp beards. Then it can be ground into a meal and used for flour or soup thickening.

Herbs

Why use herbs for healing? An understanding of their true nature will help answer that question. Herbs have a definite relationship to all other aspects of nature, including humans. The way herbs interact with people, when introduced in the form of tea, powder, or when smoked, is a result of the nature of the specific herb. All herbs differ in the way that they affect us, and we all react differently to them. Basically, one can see an herb as a "command" from the Great Spirit. An herb is an embodiment of light and the will of the Creator. When an herb is introduced to the body, the body reacts to the Creator's will or command.

An important aspect of using herbs for healing is respect. If one can see that an herb is an aspect of God's will, and is knowable—would one knowingly violate the will of the Creator? Herbs must be used as what they are—living, sensitive creatures. If they are thought of as inert, dead substances, such as the pills one buys at a drug store, they have less to give to you—because you have not given them respect.

Humans and herbs belong together. Herbs are a gentle medicine, however, and reflect this aspect of our Creator's love for us. Please be gentle with herbs and they will fill you with the love of the Creator.

As with other wild plants, herbs deserve your love and respect, especially when you're picking them. Herbs should be picked when their properties are strongest: when leaves are grown and green, when flowers are fully flowered, when roots are grown but not old and woody. If you are not sure of the time, ask the herb.

Herbs dry best in shade. When dry, they should be stored in a dark place in airtight containers so that they retain their properties.

If possible, we like to use herbs that grow nearby, especially for medicine. However, this isn't always practical as we sometimes needs herbs that don't grow locally.

There are so many useful herbs that we can't list many here, but we've chosen a few that we find helpful. For more information we again refer you to the many excellent books now available on the subject.

Alfalfa is high in vitamins and minerals, stops internal bleeding, and aids in treatment of arthritis.

Bear Tribe herbal tobacco is our own kinnikinick mixture of good herbs. It aids people who wish to stop smoking tobacco and has none of the tobacco's poisons.

Burdock root is a blood purifier, a tonic, and an aid in lung congestion.

Catnip is soothing to the nerves, especially for infants, and also reduces fevers and helps to cure colds and relieve intestinal spasm.

Cayenne pepper is a seasoning which also is used to dilate constricted blood vessels, and to help to cure colds.

Chamomile is soothing to the nerves, and is good for toothaches, earaches, and indigestion. It is also a tonic and tissue strengthener.

Comfrey leaves soothe the stomach, purify the blood, stop internal bleeding, help gallstones, headaches, cuts, and burns. Externally, they make a good poultice.

Comfrey root is a blood purifier, and also helps rheumatism, flu, gland disorders, coughs, colds, and stomach ulcers.

Echinacea was used by some tribes as a blood purifier, and to heal ulcers, infections, insect bites, abscesses, sores, and wounds.

Ephedra (Mormon, Squaw, or Indian tea) is a stimulant which can help relieve congestion and arthritis.

Goldenseal root is soothing to the mucous membranes, good for flu, skin eruptions, nose-bleeds, and sore throats. It is a tonic and an antiseptic.

Hops is a sedative and blood cleanser. It can be used to expel poison and kill worms, and to cure headaches.

Horehound breaks up congestion, helps cure coughs, lung, and throat ailments, ulcers, and is an antidote for poisons and venomous bites. It is also a laxative.

Juniper berries help to heal indigestion, coughs, skin diseases. They are also a diuretic.

Maté is a South American Native tea which is a stimulant and purgative.

Mullein helps get rid of colds and congestions, coughs, sore throats, and skin irritations.

Oregon grape root is a blood purifier and tonic, and improves digestion and skin.

Peppermint aids in stomach disorders, with heartburn, gas, and flu.

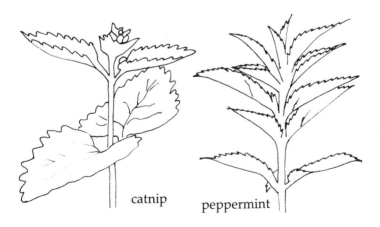

catnip   peppermint

Plantain stops external bleeding, and makes a poultice for infections, rashes, bee stings.

Raspberry leaf is used for colds, canker sores, stomach complaints, female problems, and wounds.

Rose hips are high in natural vitamin C.

Sage helps cure colds, skin disorders, and is used for purification.

Sassafras is a flavoring which purifies the blood, helps toothaches, and skin problems.

Slippery elm is used for ulcers, internal bleeding, burns, and inflamed mucous membranes.

Spearmint is a flavoring which soothes the nerves and the stomach.

Uva ursi (Bearberry, kinnikinick) is a tonic and diuretic.

Yarrow is used for colds, external and internal bleeding, flu, and fevers.

Yellow dock (Curly dock) helps with boils and other skin eruptions and with rheumatism.

Yerba santa is used for chest congestion, asthma, and, externally, for poison oak.

When we get sick we often use herbs and other natural medicines to heal ourselves.

Even with Good Medicine, it's hard to keep perfectly healthy these days. Living in an industrial country we are constant targets of chemical warfare and nuclear radiation. Hardly a day goes by that you don't see a news story about the "newly discovered" harmful effects of some food, drink, wrapping, or drug that the Food and Drug Administration has previously blessed. All the while, the defense business continues to create new forms of germs and viruses for future warfare. Some of these it seems, by reports of flu and other epidemics, sometimes slip past their protective defenses. So, if you don't live in a situation where you can grow your own food, drink only pure mountain water, breathe only fresh air, and not be exposed to people who do otherwise, it's pretty inevitable that some time during each year you'll be sick, with at least a cold or the flu.

The Bear Tribe has the same attitude toward doctors as we do toward auto mechanics. If you know just about what is wrong, what you need to get it fixed, and you can't do it yourself, then take your body to a doctor or your car to a mechanic. But if you can fix either on your own, you run a lot less risk.

We believe that doctors are good for mechanical problems—taking preventive tests, giving inoculations, setting broken bones, prescribing antibiotics for serious infections, delivering babies if home delivery seems inadvisable—but we feel that, like other mechanics, they don't have as many answers as they think they do, and they often overcharge for their advice and labor.

Consequently, we're always trying to find ways to keep our bodies functioning well, and to do minor repairs ourselves.

None of us are expert nutritionists or herbalists, but we do read what we can on the subject, and talk with people who are willing to share their expertise with us. Nor do we believe that herbs are the only good method of treatment. Like homeopaths (like cures like) we feel that small quantities of any drug or substance that gets your natural defenses working is good. There have been times when we've felt our own defenses were weak enough that we've used normal quantities of antibiotics or decongestants. But the side effects of such drugs have proven bad enough that we avoid doing so if at all possible.

Here we'd like to share with you some of the cures that we've actually used for colds, flus, and minor infections with good results. We don't promise these cures will benefit you in any way, but they have helped some of us. If you are pregnant, dealing with a small child, or seriously ill, you should, of course, see a body mechanic.

The cold is one common and annoying sickness that can sometimes respond well to home care. If you are getting slight sniffles and take one gram of vitamin C (preferably organic) four to ten times a day, that may be enough. If it isn't, the best cure we've discovered is *chewing* (don't just swallow) one large clove of organic garlic in the morning, and one at night. If you chew some parsley afterwards, it gets rid of the taste. If you still can't stand the taste, try cutting a small garlic clove into tiny pieces, putting it in a cup, and mashing it. Add the juice of one-quarter small lemon. Brew a cup of herb tea—mint is good—and add the garlic, lemon, and some honey. Let it sit three minutes. Drink a cup three times a day until the cold is gone. We've cured bad colds that have gone to the throat or ears in four days, using this method. Sun Bear's favorite cold remedy is hot apple cider vinegar and honey tea, which is made by adding a cup of boiling water to two to three tablespoons of vinegar and as much honey as you need to make it drinkable. Some of us substitute lemon juice for vinegar in this recipe.

Another herbal cure we've used for colds, flus, and other infections caught in the early stages is our herbal infection mixture, consisting of one part goldenseal powder, to two parts each of myrrh and echinacea powder. This really tastes bad, so we put it in large-size capsules and take three or four each day. If you can rest as soon as you feel a cold or flu coming on, that helps a lot. So does a long, tepid, soaking bath. Also be conscious of not exposing other people to your mucus.

Teas that we've found to help cure colds and flu are yarrow, comfrey leaf, and chamomile mixed together. We usually put a tablespoon of each in about a quart of boiling water, and let steep for twenty minutes. If this is all you'll be using for a home cure make it medicine strength, which is one tablespoon of the mixture to one cup of water. We have also used ephedra (squaw) tea to relieve nasal congestion.

If we have a fever with a flu we sometimes take large capsules filled with cayenne pepper (capsicum). The cayenne helps us to sweat more profusely, which gets rid of the toxins in our body so the fever can break. We sometimes also take a cayenne capsule followed by some lemon juice before we take our sweats, as this causes us to sweat more and get rid of more toxic matter. Cayenne does speed up your heart and circulation, so be cautious if you have any heart problems. Some tribal medicine people use sweats to make a fever run its course quicker. We don't recommend that a lay person use this method. Instead, use cold baths or alcohol rubs given every fifteen to thirty minutes until the fever is down, or sponge the person off with cool cloths. In between coolings, be sure the person is covered well so they don't chill.

For teas to combat a fever, take peppermint and elder flower (or yarrow) tea made by adding two cups of boiling water to one-quarter ounce of elder flowers (or yarrow). Drink, then go to bed. The tea works by opening the pores so the toxins can come out. This is okay for children. Medicine-strength sage tea is also good. If the fever is 104 degrees Fahrenheit or higher it is *dangerous*, and you'd better get to a doctor fast.

For stomach flu (or food poisoning) the quickest cure we've found is taking large capsules of goldenseal powder, along with vitamin C. We've taken them every hour or two for up to eight hours, and been rid of all the flu symptoms by then. When we have stomach flu, we don't try to eat until we feel like it, and we usually start off with citrus fruit. Peppermint, chamomile, and comfrey tea, separately or together, seem to settle the stomach. You can also try vinegar and honey tea for stomach pain or flu.

Remember that often what we consider colds or other illnesses are really the body cleansing itself of the toxins (poisons) it can't handle. Heavy medication will suppress the symptoms without really helping effect a cure. When your body is trying to clean itself out the best thing you can do is help it by fasting or eating only lightly, taking an enema if you know how to properly, drinking herb teas to cleanse the kidneys, sweating, bathing in hot then cold water, and using dry body massage with a rough cloth or luffa to cleanse the skin. Sleeping is good as the body can often work better if we're not disturbing it. Don't do any of the things we've suggested unless they feel right to you and your body. Remember, more natural methods of healing often take longer than chemicals. Be patient and listen to your body. Respect it and consider it worthy of healing. Pray for whatever healing is supposed to come to you. Picture yourself as healthy again. If you don't feel comfortable using natural healing, don't let someone else convince you that you do. Go to a doctor.

In an emergency situation, a visualization technique can help until you can get medical aid. In a reassuring, positive tone of voice, let the victim know that you are there to help him, then direct him to close his eyes. Place your fingers or palm very lightly on the injured spot and tell the victim to focus his attention on the touch of your hand. Change the position of where you are touching him and repeat this instruction. For best results, apply your touch to areas which are further from his head than the pain area.

Speak positively but not excessively. As you touch him briefly, spot after spot, direct him to put his attention on the feeling of your touch. If there is any trembling or pain experienced, keep up the treatments for several minutes, even up to an hour, if necessary, until most of the pain has been relieved. At this time the victim may be directed to apply his own touch to these areas, and thereby aid himself.

Normally, there is pain and slow recovery with injuries, sprains, burns, headaches, and colds as the victim is avoiding the "hurt" area with his vital energy. Although it may seem otherwise, it is not the power from your finger which aids him; it is his own vital force that he generates by focusing on the touch of your hand on his body. All you are doing is placing him in communication with the injury, which allows him to send his own vital force to the spot in order to promote healing and stop the pain. Needless to say, if there is any first aid equipment or help available, it is to be used along with this technique.

In cases where you are alone, this technique is just as effective. Instead of talking to the victim, talk to yourself and apply the touching system on your own body. Allow yourself the realization that the vital healing force is there; all you have to do is to direct it by focusing on the right spot. Normally, this force flows naturally to all parts of the body, thus keeping one in good health. However, in the case of a sudden injury, pain may create fear, panic, and shock which results in the mental blockage of this force.

If you are planning either to live in the wilderness or to be in situations working with a lot of people, we strongly recommend that you do as we have and take a course in cardiopulmonary resuscitation (CPR) each year. It does save lives. We also recommend taking the emergency first aid courses given by the Red Cross. These courses give you both techniques and confidence in your ability to help in an emergency.

Eating

"Our old food we used to eat was good. The meat from the buffalo and game was good. It made us strong. These cows are good to eat, soft, tender, but they are not like that meat. Our people used to live a long time. Today we eat white man's food, we cannot live so long—maybe seventy, maybe eighty years, not a hundred. Sweet Medicine told us that. He said this food would be sweet, and after we taste this food we want it, and forget our own foods. Chokecherries and plums and wild turnips and honey from the wild bees, that was our food. This other food is too sweet. We eat it and forget . . . It's all coming true, what he said." Fred Last Bull, Keeper of the Sacred Arrows of the Cheyenne Tribe, told that to an audience in Busby, Montana, in 1967.

We feel that Sweet Medicine's words of prophecy are true, and that more people every day are becoming aware of the possibility that the food they are eating to sustain them may, in reality, be killing them.

Each day we see the Food and Drug Administration raise new issues about the safety and purity of the food we eat. First it was breakfast cereals, then cyclamates, then red dye #2, which was used in just about everything. When the FDA decertified red dye #2 it didn't mean it was off the shelves. Manufacturers had to stop producing it, but they were allowed to sell their inventories. Then red dye #40, which was used to replace #2, was also suspected of causing cancer. Preservatives are also exceptionally harmful in food. Sodium nitrate used, again, in just about everything, produces changes in cell structure and may cause cancer. BHA and BHT, petroleum products used to preserve many other foods, cause a reduced growth weight, liver problems, and fetal abnormalities. Stilbestrol, a hormone popular for fattening up cattle, causes the meat to be mostly water fat, not protein, and can cause breast cancer and fibroid tumors in women, sterility and impotence in men, and arrested growth in children. In late 1970, the FDA doubled the amount of stilbestrol allowed in cattle feed. In the

161

1980s, despite much public protest, they also allowed food to be treated with radiation because it is alleged to reduce spoilage. We could go on, but you probably get the idea.

What can we do? We all have to eat, and most of us can't afford to buy only health food products and game. What we have done is try to balance our budget with the knowledge we have about nutrition and about the things that are particularly harmful, with no redeeming qualities.

White flour and white sugar, from all reputable reports, seem to be of no value to our bodies. So we try to substitute wheat flour and honey whenever possible. If someone gives us a bag of white flour we don't throw it away, but we use it in combination with wheat.

We try to grow as much of our fruits and vegetables as possible. We recycle things we can't eat for compost, we don't use organic sprays, and we put a lot of love into our garden. In return we get natural foods, safe from pesticides and hormones. As we've said in the past, it is feasible for most everyone to have a garden these days, to help your budget as well as your body. Even in the city, you can find vacant lots or backyards where you can plant a small garden. To preserve our fruits and vegetables for the months when they can't grow, we dry or can them. Remember to check out abandoned orchards, or orchards where you can pick things yourself, and ask the grower whether or not he uses pesticides. Organic fruit is better, but so hard to get these days that we use other fruit, and peel it or wash it well.

Sprouts are a good, year-round way of getting vitamin C and minerals. They are easily made with alfalfa seeds, lentils, wheat, and other grains and seeds. Start with organic seeds, put them in a jar, let them stand in water for about eight hours, drain, wash, and rinse them with water three or four times a day for the next three days. By the fourth day they should be fairly sprouted. Rinse them, then put them in the sun for a day so their chlorophyll will come out, bag them, and refrigerate them until you use them in salads, eggs, soups, stews, almost anything.

To get unadulterated meats, we not only raise our own animals but also make our own feed. If you buy commercial chicken feed, for instance, you get just about all the hormones that commercial chicken farmers do. If you raise your own chickens, using feed you've made, you're also fairly certain of getting good, fresh eggs.

For those of you who can't raise your own meat, we suggest looking into small animal raising operations in your area. In some places you can get organic chicken or rabbit meat if you ask around. It's also possible to buy beef directly from a rancher before the cow has been sent to the feed lots for its hormone-fattening diet. Some butchers do sell wild game, and buffalo or venison are a great beef substitute when available.

We often substitute vegetarian dishes for meat, and this alternative is available to anyone, wherever they live. When you make vegetarian dishes it is important to get a complete protein, which is done by the correct combination of grains, cheese, beans, legumes, etc.

We meet our dairy needs with a cow or goats. For those of you not fortunate enough to be able to have one, we suggest checking small dairies or health food stores for raw cow or goat milk. From it, you can make your own butter, yogurt, and cottage cheese fairly easily at home. If you prefer the prices of nonfat skim milk, find out how it is produced. The spray drying method does not destroy food value, while the roller drying method, which requires high heating, causes destruction of protein and vitamins.

We usually check out natural food co-ops or go directly to farmers, preferably organic, for our wheat, rice, lentils, etc. If you can get together with some friends and buy in bulk quantities, you can get much better prices on these items, as well as on fruits and vegetables.

What you eat can drastically affect how you feel, think, and look. We feel that taking the extra time to get and cook foods that will help to keep us in good condition is one of the best investments we can make.

To eat well, it is essential that food is prepared, served, and eaten with prayers and love. People in negative states should not cook, as their attitudes can poison the food. People on "food trips," be they vegetarians, macrobiotic, fruitarian, meat only, or whatever, often get angry if their particular demands are not being met. Such people should be kept out of the kitchen until they learn to respect other people's feelings on food. We have found that people who make diet their religion have a difficult time living in groups that don't agree with them. However, we now have people of all food persuasions living together harmoniously. The secret? Love, respect, patience, and the ability to close one's mouth.

In the kitchen, it's also helpful to practice self-reliance. Experiment. Don't become dependent on recipe books. If you're not exactly sure how to make something, use your intuition. As long as there is love in your heart, you'll do fine.

Finances

We feel sad and frustrated each time we see people forced to give up their plans of building a home in the country. Usually they have to return to town and look for a job. To us, it means that those people have ended up paying into an economic system without gaining the reward they sought. Somebody else profited from their mistake. In addition, the people who were caught in that trap will probably become discouraged and find it more difficult to try again. A little more financial planning could have saved their home, their plans, and their dreams. It is important to have a realistic idea of what to expect, and be prepared for it.

Rising costs are not just a city problem. Everything you will need will cost something in terms of cash, transportation, time, or labor. Gasoline alone will cost a substantial amount, and whether you now believe it or not, there will be unexpected but necessary trips to town with a vehicle.

The throwaway society we have grown up in has made it too much a habit to be wasteful. We seem to have lost many of the old skills of economizing. Our grandparents who lived through the Great Depression were magicians at recycling, reusing, saving, and just plain using less in the first place. Chicken bones were saved for broth, and it was unnecessary to buy instant soups. Little chips of leftover soap were collected to be used again in a draw-string bag made of two wash cloths. Socks were darned. (See if you can find anyone who knows how to darn.) Fabric scraps were saved for quilts and patches. The amount and variety of items that were saved and used again was impressive.

The breakneck pace of living now makes it attractive to do many things the expedient way. There is room for conveniences, and it is important to count human energy, too, when we figure cost. For a family trying to make a start in a self-reliant life-style, but still having to keep a job, it is brutal to insist that they must wash their own clothes by hand because a laundromat is too waste-ful. The time and energy they save by using machines in that instance can be better spent winterizing a house or salvaging lum-

164

ber. The point is to be conscious of the cost of everything, so your choices will serve you better.

Learn to expect the unexpected. There will be flat tires, broken-down equipment from time to time, injured livestock in need of veterinary attention, incidental expenses in building, and personal needs. When your vehicle needs attention, it behooves you to repair it as soon as possible, on a priority basis. You will find that being without it slows down or stops your work. You may be able to get by without it later, but while you are still learning to be self-reliant you will need it for materials, feed, food, firewood, trash, fertilizer, road maintenance, people, and critters.

Budgeting can be a pain in the neck. However, our attitude is that your budget is your friend. There is little way of planning your spending and when it will occur unless you take this step. It is, therefore, impossible to plan your income. Budgeting is also a way of seeing what you can afford, and when, and how much the alternatives will cost. If you have a car but need a truck, write down your alternatives. Your car is paid for. But to move enough two-by-fours to frame your house will take thirty trips to town in your car. How much does that cost? You could rent a truck for two days. How much does that cost? Is there anything else you can use the truck for at the same time? How much will you save later by doing that? How much is your car worth? Is there a market for it? How much would it cost to buy a truck? And how much does it cost to run either one? Is a truck useful for all your needs, or would you be constantly adding gas to an empty truck that only gets fifteen miles to the gallon? These questions can be answered only when you have taken the time to realistically budget it out. Keep your work sheets. Write down your conclusions. This information will be available when you need it later.

Here are examples of very fictional budgets. *You will have to check local prices and availability each year.*

Home Insulation

Insulate to R38 with Fiberglas	$1,000.00	(depending on the size of the house)
Insulate to R19 with less Fiberglas	$ 650.00	
You have "saved"	$ 350.00	

But now you have to get your firewood.

Firewood for a home with R19 (10 cords of pine $\times$ $60.00) = $600.00

Firewood for a home with R38 (4 cords of pine $\times$ $60.00) = $240.00

By using the cheaper way of insulating you saved $350.00, but you have had to spend an additional $360.00 for wood, in one year only. You could have "paid for" the extra insulation in just one season by using less wood. You are probably still cold and need another woodshed which will cost another $40.00 to build, if you're very careful.

Firewood for Heating

Pine $60.00 per cord, no delivery
   8.00 to drive your own vehicle to pick up the wood,
   _____ one cord at a time
  $68.00 for three weeks of heat. This equals $23.00 per week.
$23.00 × 25 (the number of weeks you must heat) = $575.00 per year.

Birch $90.00 per cord, delivered
   no cost for pickup
  $90.00 for *six* weeks of heat. This equals $15.00 per week.
$15.00 × 25 (the number of weeks you must heat) = $375.00 per year.

Cost of heating for one year with pine	$575.00
Cost of heating for one year with birch	375.00
Savings from getting the "expensive" wood	$200.00

Getting Your Own Firewood

First check to see if you need a permit to allow you to cut wood on government land. In most cases this is a fire regulation because of the increased potential for fire when chainsaws and vehicles are brought into a wooded area. If you need a permit it will cost about $10.00, which is not much.

  Now let's be idealistic and say you have a truck, a pickup with relatively decent mileage. And you must go 50 miles to cut wood. 50 miles in an empty truck ÷ 17 miles per gallon of gasoline = 2.94 gallons. At $1.00 a gallon:

Cost of gasoline for empty truck	$2.94
Motor oil and wear and tear	3.00
Gasoline for a full truck (12 mi./gal.)	4.17
Permit	10.00
Cost of driving only	$20.11

Cost of a reconditioned chainsaw, hypothetically $295.00
Cost of a new chainsaw with a guarantee $359.99

Cost of chainsaw oil ($1.79/qt. × 2 qts.) $3.58
Five gallons of gasoline for the chainsaw   5.00
    $8.58

    Let's say you bought the new chainsaw with the guarantee, to save on repairs, and you are able to use it to cut 15 cords of wood, replacing only a $35.00 chain.

Cost of chainsaw $359.99
Chain replacement   30.00
    $389.99
    ÷ 15 cords
    $26.00 cost of chainsaw per cord

    So far, here are the costs:

Cost of driving $ 20.11
Chainsaw per cord   26.00 first cord
    26.00 second cord
    $ 72.11 for the trip
    ÷ 2 cords of pine
    $ 36.05 per cord for pine

    You have spent two hours driving and six hours cutting and loading wood. You have saved $47.90, and it took eight hours. Was it worth it?
    Such financial hypothesizing can help you to determine real costs, which often vary greatly from apparent costs.

Insurance

Insurance is a good idea, and a necessity for anyone buying a home, a homestead, or a farm on mortgage. We lost our poultry in a fire one year, and our insurance was very helpful when we rebuilt our flock. It would have been difficult, otherwise, to recoup our losses. Take a good look at any insurance you buy, and weigh the likelihood of your needing it. Insurance is extremely costly these days, and unnecessary insurance can really drain your finances. Be sure to know what coverage you're buying. It is a bitter disappointment to have spent thousands of dollars on insurance, only to find that it does not cover your loss, or that the deductible is so large that you, in essence, are paying the whole bill yourself.

If you purchase medical insurance, shop carefully. Many different kinds are available. They are all expensive, but so are medical emergencies. One alternative to normal insurance, which has proven to be effective for some people and groups, is self-insurance. This means religiously setting aside a certain amount of money in a savings account you don't touch unless there is the kind of emergency you would usually depend upon insurance to pay.

Other Financial Realities

You will need to pay for your supplies, be they for building or for generating income. Lumber, nails, roofing, insulation, concrete footings, wiring for electricity are all becoming more expensive. Seed for crops, feed for livestock, veterinary supplies can all take big bites out of your budget.

Unless you have vast financial resources readily available, you will need a reliable source of income. Get at least part of that happening before you move to the country, and be sure it works. Do not depend on anything that hasn't yet become reality.

In the fairly recent past, there have been some attempts on the part of federal and local government to provide services to people feeling the financial pinch. These attempts have not borne much fruit, as far as we have seen, though they were all good ideas. We found that the weatherization programs were so short of money that they had to be limited to the very elderly. The SBA (Small Business Administration) provides a great deal of common sense advice, but no specific information, and very little funding. You'd be better off to write a grant for a research project. Local food banks can only give what they have. If all they have is fourteen cases of saltines, that's what they give out. Food stamps are more or less expensive, depending on your eligibility, but undermine your self-reliance. If you honestly qualify, do use them while you must, but know that their value is limited compared to what you can do for yourself. Likewise, unemployment can be a large expenditure of time and energy. If you need the income, it is better to stay employed as long as you need the income, or change your occupation to one you can do while you're building your self-reliant home base.

We recommend you take a close look at what it costs to do the things you want to do. Financing is complicated, compared to the old days when a person paid his money and took the goods. When you look carefully at loans and financing, you find that the interest, no matter how low, is the real moneymaker for banks. Ask specific questions, such as "When I make my first payment of $300, how much of that money pays interest, and how much pays principal?" The answer could be shocking.

If you must borrow money, go in with your eyes wide open. What happens if your payment is late? What if interest rates go down? Can you refinance? Is there an early payoff figure? If you are ahead in making your payments, do you still have to pay every month, or can you skip one month? You might find you'd be better off to save the money and pay it when it's due.

All this means that you will have to find income which doesn't cut too badly into the time you must spend getting your shelter together before winter. If you are lucky, you will have money coming in from something you did in the past, like writing a best seller or buying an oil well. But for most of us this is not the case, and we have to develop an industry to keep us in the chips.

Spending should be done carefully. If you have cash, you are in a better position to bargain for what you buy. Still, be sure you are getting a good deal. Scout out secondhand items. Carefully check out things that need repair. It might get you in deeper than you meant to be. Sometimes you will have to buy something new. Wait for a sale, if you can.

Do not count on trading for everything. Trading is only now becoming popular, and it still takes some looking to find a taker for your goods who has anything you are interested in. Trading can take up a lot of your time, although trade organizations help to make it more feasible.

If you have a phone, keep the bill paid. Keep up your land payment, if you have one. Delinquency charges set people back far enough so they frequently fail to recover. Interest charges on accounts are astounding. It's best to always pay cash. But someday you might need credit, and you will want to be considered a good credit risk. Pay your taxes so the county won't auction off your tax-delinquent land.

Some of the things which can be done to generate income are cutting and delivering firewood (which requires an investment of time and money in chainsaws, gas, and incidentals and is pretty seasonal), selling produce (which again, is seasonal, and you need a whole lot of it), and selling eggs. Selling milk will come under the jurisdiction of the state department of agriculture. Selling most food items comes under many rules and regulations from health department inspectors and the FDA. This kind of industry should be successfully operating fully before you move it to the country. Remember that more of your time will be spent in getting back and forth once you're on the land. Keeping bees and selling honey, raising and selling earthworms, harvesting and selling herbs, baking and selling pies and cakes, making candy, and making sprouts are all ways to bring in some income. But unless you'll be doing any of these on a large scale you'll need some other kind of cottage industry to support you.

Home Industries

Home industries are a boon to self-reliance, but you have to work at them as regularly and conscientiously as you would at any other job. This should not be difficult for, after all, you are working toward your own gain, and not someone else's. You should try to have some organized space just for the industries you develop, and certain time in the week just for working on these.

You should be producing goods for which there is a demand. You should try to produce a quality item at a minimum of expense, both in money and in labor. Your time will be valuable, so do not spend too many hours on items which sell slowly. Remember that most people must economize, and you will have to keep your cost as reasonable as possible, but do not sell your time too cheaply.

Marketing is important. Unless you have friends with an outlet for selling your products fairly rapidly, you will have to do a little legwork yourself. You will have to find out what people buy best, and try to make your products appealing to them. Some items sell best in boutiques, some at fairs, and some through mail order. Try all these possibilities.

Keep good records of your business. Keep caught up. Nothing is worse than botched up bookkeeping and filing. If you owe money, pay it. If someone else owes you, collect it. But you can do these things well only if you follow good, ethical business practices.

Sewing is a creative industry, but find out what items are popular. Usually, people will not buy what they think they can do themselves. That reduces your chances of making it on potholders and quilts and toys. In some places, denim clothing is popular, and articles made from "worn" denim can be remade according to current styles. Materials can be bought at thrift stores for long skirts, chair seats, hats, bags, baby slings, jackets, tool aprons, and other things.

Outdoor articles are more in demand than they were ten years ago, and money can be made from custom-making sleeping bags, tipis, day packs, and containers and covers for various items. It is best to fill orders, so that your materials are not all sewn up in things that aren't being sold. This means you may have to advertise in a couple of classified sections.

Also consider leather work, such as making moccasins, purses, shirts, pants, jackets. These are all good, useful products that will help others as well as your finances. If you have access to hides, tanning them and selling them is another way of making money.

Another creative, sometimes lucrative industry is furniture making—and you can make any number of things. Chairs, tables, bureaus, desks, lofts, redwood tubs can all be made and sold. If you prefer to work on a smaller scale, you can construct children's furniture, doll furniture, or even toys. We've met people who make their money doing all of these things.

Jewelry making is another way of getting finances together. You can make beaded items or silver, metal, copper, or gold ones. You can also make pillows, pillow furniture, stuffed toys, quilts, stoneware, and ceramics.

When you're planning a cottage industry your imagination, your craft work inclinations, what will sell, and how you'll sell it are the things you must consider.

Trading

Who needs money?

The old-timers lived happily without it for many thousands of years. They built their own shelters, grew or hunted for their food, made their clothes and weapons, and traded for whatever goods they could not produce, or services they couldn't perform.

With cities and middlemen came the need for money, checkbooks, credit, and all of the other civilized abstractions that keep us from remembering the true value of both goods and services. Today, many people are trying to turn away from money and conduct their business by barter. This concept has become popular enough that there are barter companies in several large cities that arrange trades for their big money clients who recognize the advantages of trading.

We've been trading, whenever possible, for many years. We believe that learning to trade is an important first step in creating a viable economic alternative to the system while it exists, and that trading will replace money after the cleansing. We've traded turquoise jewelry for beadwork, beads, blankets, baskets, feathers, pottery, pictures, and leather work; then we've turned around and traded some or all of those items for turquoise. Which way we traded depended upon what we had more of at one time, and what we needed. We've also traded arts and crafts for dental work, medical help, foodstuffs, and herbs. We've traded our labor picking fruit for part of the fruit we've picked. We've had people pay back money loans by working on our magazine. We partially paid people working on our mailing list with a wool blanket. We've taken soybeans and beads in trade for subscriptions.

If you watch children trading baseball cards or water pistols you'll see that trading can, and should, be a lot of fun and more satisfying than dealing in pictures of dead presidents. Probably half our trade deals so far have been for the pure joy of the give and take of a trade. The other half enabled us to get items we needed with no cash outlay. We've made some terrific trade deals at pow-wows and shows, largely because of our willingness to trade. There are some rules we try to follow to make all of our trades happy ones, and we pass them on to you.

1. Never agree to a trade unless you are completely happy with it. There should be no thoughts of exchanges or refunds in a trade.

2. Don't ever let anyone push you into a trade. As trading grows, so does the possibility of con people who will try to get rid of their junk through trading.

3. Conversely, don't ever try to push someone else into a trade. Some people just aren't financially able to trade at this time. For instance, many Indian silversmiths can't afford to trade their goods because the people who sell them raw materials demand cold cash for these materials.

4. If you think the other person is making a bad trade through ignorance of the items being traded, tell him. If he still wants to go ahead, that's his business.

5. For a trade to make both parties happy, they both have to feel that they are the one who has done just a bit better. Always be willing to throw in that last little item to make the other person feel that they have the edge. One happy trade between two people will usually lead to others.

A problem that we still encounter in trades is having to assign a dollar value to items in order to judge whether the trade is fair. For instance, when we traded with our dentist he billed us full charge for his services, then he picked out the items he wanted and we billed him for those. We are so conditioned to think of value in terms of money that it is hard to break the habit, but if we were stuck for a while in the country with a toothache, and a dentist came along and said he'd fix it if we gave him a squash-blossom necklace, we bet we wouldn't think too much about what the necklace has cost us. When we have to trade for need as well as fun, then we will begin to attach real value to things again. To a starving man, a loaf of bread will be worth a brick of gold.

The best, probably only, way to learn to trade is by trading. To get in some practice go to a powwow, Indian, antique, or collectors show, a flea market or countercultural fair and see how you do. Once you feel comfortable at trading, try it wherever you think there's any possibility it might work. If it doesn't you haven't lost anything. If it does you've converted another person to taking it out in trade.

Trade organizations are a good way to introduce people to trading, and to expand the scope of trades you can make. The trade organization we belong to works like this. We pay a monthly cash fee to cover their postage, phone bills, etc. If we need printing done, we find out if a member printer can do our job. If he does, he gives us an invoice for the regular cost. Our account shows we owe credits for printing. Then someone may call us for turquoise, firewood, or an ad in *Wildfire*, and we bill them and get credit for what we sold. The advantages are that we don't have to find a direct trade, and consequently, have access to many more materials and services through trading.

Harmony

One of the blessings of leaving the city and getting a rural home is that many hassles cease to be. Your energy can be directed to real building and real achievement for your own gain. The newness of lifestyle may lead some people to think that all controls may be dropped, but we have found that attitude to be naive and unwise. It ultimately saves time, worry, and even money to "keep it together" with the law and the neighbors.

Motor Vehicles

Keep all your vehicles in legal shape. Keep them in safe operating condition. Headlights should work, and so should windshield wipers, muffler, horn, etc. Some state laws require certain tires or chains during the winter. Know what they are. If your car is stopped, you will be given a notice to repair anything that doesn't work. You may also get fined.

Make sure that only licensed drivers operate your vehicle. Insurance is a good idea, even if it isn't mandatory. A vehicle can be an asset or a pain in the neck. Keep it together.

Building Codes

Counties can interfere if you seem to be building without a permit. They can issue a stop work order. If you violate an order, the legal consequences will be very serious and will cripple anything else you try to do. It is easier to just buy the permit. The same goes for electric and septic permits.

Use of Firearms

Do not hunt, under any circumstances, if you don't need to. If you have other things under control, you probably won't need to. But if you do, get the license, even though you might feel negative about it. If you poach and get caught, it will be a sorry day indeed.

Some ordinances prohibit the discharge of firearms within certain zones and within certain distances of dwellings. If you have firearms, become familiar with local laws pertaining to them and carefully observe them.

School-Age Children

If you have school-age children and you object to sending them to public school, be equipped to provide a decent alternative. School authorities can come and test the children at any time, to be sure they are learning a standard amount and type of matter. If you keep children out of school without providing an adequate education (private tutoring, homebound studies, or whatever the local law requires) there is a risk of the children being removed from the "unfit" home.

Drugs

Don't use them. While the legal hassles they cause are nasty, the other things they do to people are even worse.

Zoning

If you are moving into a new area, scout around and find out whether outhouses are forbidden by law. Also find out whether or not you will be free to raise livestock. If you live in an irrigation district, learn the regulations. If you don't learn them, not only will the law be on your tail, but so will all your neighbors.

Campfires, Fishing

Don't ask for trouble. If you don't *know* it's all right, don't do it. It is never good to flaunt the law. If you're sure it's all right to fish, take only what you need, and be prepared to show your license to any fish and game personnel who might check on you. Most campfires need a permit, and they are usually free, so it is stupid not to get one if it is required.

Critters

A little awareness and consideration will keep most people out of trouble with the wildlife. Do not try to approach animals or capture them. Friends can be made of them without domestication. Go to extra measures to avoid their homes and areas during mating and baby animal seasons. Avoid rabies-carrying species at all times. Do not touch or handle dead animals. Remove their bodies with a shovel, and bury them away from children and your own pets.

Folks

If you move to the country, you might have neighbors in the area. They will probably resent your being there, since they probably moved to be away from people, the same as you. They were there first, so you will have to be on your best behavior to keep from alienating them further. They will appreciate it if you keep to yourself and mind your own business. Avoid asking favors and borrowing things. Keep your noise level down. Keep your area clean and free of eyesores. At first, your neighbors will wish you would go away, and some will even try to drive you away. Don't give them the excuse they are looking for. A good relationship can always develop. Don't be too eager to be there to help, but be ready to combat fire or share road maintenance. This is a real part of your responsibility anyway. Keep your animals out of the neighbor's garden. Don't trespass or let your guests trespass because they don't know where the property lines are. Respect the water supply. Keep your business to yourself.

V

Poetry and Legends

Poetry

O Great Spirit
Sun, Moon, Sky, and Sea;
You are inside,
And all around me.

Your Breath comes so gently,
It sweeps across the land.
It blows with such power,
To heal our fellow man.

Your eyes are upon us,
From ourselves we cannot hide.
We must move with our changes,
As with the changing tide.

Thank you for your beauty.
Thank you for this life.
Teach us to follow
The path of your Light.

O Great Spirit,
We greet you with our love,
We yearn for your wisdom,
The blessings of your love.
Lend us your guiding love.

O Great Spirit,
Sun, Moon, Sky and Sea;
You are inside,
And all around me.

—Thanks to Antahkarana
for this song

Listen . . .

Sometimes
I long
to shout—
"Stop! Stop
the slaughter
of our Mother
and of the good
and bountiful
beauty upon Her!"

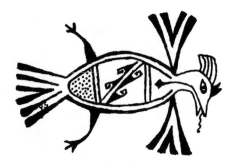

this longing,
this voice—
within was given
to me by the Great Spirit.
It is the voice
of love.

Be silent.
Listen.
From the silence
within yourself
you will
hear it too.

It is a roar.
It is a whisper.
And it is ever
present—
waiting to guide
you, if only
you will listen.

The Voice
will reveal
to you
to respect
your little brothers,
the beauty creatures,
and to preserve
the plant and water
nations.

From it,
you will learn
the friendliness
of trees
and not to curse
the rain.
Walk in the rain
and be thankful
for its goodness.

Give thanks,
when our Mother
turns Her colors—
season to season;
they are beautiful
each in their own
way and we
also turn and change
spinning out part
in the cycle.

You will learn
that you
do not need

so many things
and gadgets
that you are killing
yourselves and your
Mother to obtain.

Everything you need
has been provided.
It is here—
the Voice
will tell
you—
if only you will
listen—

—Wi i ni napa

Brother of Darkness

I rise up before you
to beckon, taunt, and poke
you toward the doorway of darkness
that I Raven am.

Why do you fear so the darkness I am?
Do you not see the richness
there between the stars in which I revel
or feel the glory, the strength, the life in me?
It is all of darkness.

I am an evil that throbs and breathes
like a dark animal.
Wrap it around you like a fur blanket.
It has an odor of musk
the weight of a bear ready to hibernate.

I have come to guide you
to the dark underworld of your midnight—
the black diamond
hidden within your heart.

Take my mantle of darkness over your head
like a cobra's hood. See the satin, iridescence
of my black outstretched wings in the night.
Fly with me over the cities into alleys
filled with the garbage of day,
onto the beaches barren with torment, pain
and negation of life.

My darkness has no negation in it.
There is nothing there to see we cannot accept.
Follow me into the heart of your darkness.
Plunge into that dark cave.
Invite each fear to rise and follow after the last.
With my straight beak we shall poke into the entrails
of each fear to see the dark creature who sleeps there
beneath the leaves of denial
in the sterile cave of fear.

As long as you cling to your light, the strength
that is spring will not rise up in you.
Taste the exotic flavor of each fear.
Know each fear is a forsaken friend hungry for your hand.
Feel your friend's embrace absorb and enfold your loneliness.

Belong to the darkness as I belong to it.
I offer you a pathway of night
Plunge into this night
as you would a warm lake
where there is no light to reveal your nakedness.

In this cave of completion, the marriage of light and darkness
will be consummated: winter and summer will be wed.
The full circle of your soul will enclose all life;
then you shall know no barrenness.

—Eleanor Limmer

Small Daughter . . .
Hold my drum
over the fire a moment
Then we will sing
Your Mother's song . . .   —Frank Chilcote

Seven Drummers

Seven drummers sang
a really good song
not too fast
but fast enough
to make everyone
feel good

two or three
at a time
the dancers went out
each one moving
in their own
graceful way

one man was dancing
along with all
the rest
he had smooth
graceful rhythm
he was straight
and tall

he moved slow
to start
his broad shoulders
dipping one
at a time
in slow circles

his head bobbing
slightly in
time with
the drum
and all the while
his body swayed
from side to side

he moved in deep
among the dancers
circling the drum
like all the rest
he was straight

and tall
when he danced
past the children
he knew they
were watching
(for this he danced
proud)

as the drum
beat faster
he danced faster
and more skillfully
dust began to rise
from the thickly
matted grass

deeper still inside
the circle he danced
he danced around
two young men₁
a challenge to
contest they
would not take

he danced behind
a young girl
then next to her
finally he slowed
and danced in place
in front of her

he danced slow
and graceful
straight and tall
when the drumming
stopped he stopped
he stood motionless

proud and silent
listening to the
echoing bells of
dancers who didn't
know the song
as well as he did

—R. A. SwanSon
Ojibwe Poet

The Drums Touch

Drum beats
•Heart beats
Hoof beats
Drum beat meets
Heart beat

Vibrations tell all
Listen
To the heart beat
Listen
To the hoof beat

Drums touch brings
The sound of
Skin on skin
Stretched over cedar
Stretched over bone

Hoof beat
Heart beat
Drum beat
Blend into
One

Hoof beats give life
To become drumbeats
Drumbeats bring life
To the
Heart

—R. A. SwanSon
Ojibwe Poet

Circles of Life

Child of Mine, let us sit together
    in a Circle of Two 'round the Fire.
Grandmother Moon peeks at us
    rising up from the Wilderness,
    gliding 'round beyond the Mountains.

It is a Good Night, the Loon Wails.

We shall talk of the Womb, Little Sister,
    it is Time you should know
    how it Comes and Goes, rising and emptying
    for the Little Ones yet to be Born.

Small as your fist: circular, small tight sphere,
    glistening in the deep dark
    never yet prepared for Landings,
        nor shed itself in the Absence of them.
Yours is empty and quiet as yet.

For a few days a Nest is my Womb,
    of Red, dear, not White like our Relative;
Mine lies full, like Grandma up there.

Yours too will fill with vast nourishments
    to empty Life's Bright Red River
    trickling toward the Light of Sun.

Then the quiet time, while other Growings carry on,
    when Roots grow Strong and
    the egg grows silently and
    Moon goes Invisibly on her path.

Smoke with me, Child, there is more to come.

What stops this great Silent Rhythm?
How does it Cease, then to Resume?

Circles, Child, two Circles
    becoming One Circle to Grow
        to two, alike yet so unlike
            to grow to four and eight and so on and on,
                to Fill the Nest.
        Nine Moons filling the Great Circle
        Then to Push on Out, Another of Life's Rivers
        Meeting the glare of Sun and growing
            on the Air and Soil of Mother Earth.

The Red River trickles on, cleansing the now-stretched sphere;
    again, and again, and again.

Forever you ask?

Be Still, Child, the Moon comes, the Loon Calls.

You are soon to have your Beginnings:
    the End of your Childhood of Freedom.

I am soon to have my Ending,
    the Beginning of my Final Freedoms . . .

Circles, Child of Mine, Circles 'round the Fire.

—Morning Star

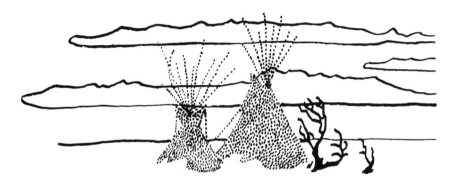

Legends

How the Bear Clan Became the Medicine Clan

The morning was still and calm. A few birds sang their welcome to the growing light. Some smoke rose curling from the lodges scattered about the clearing. A small stream from behind the lodges added its voice to the morning song. Now and then a door flap would open and a woman would emerge, face East for a moment, then go about her day fetching wood for fires, or dipping water for her cooking needs.

As the light grew stronger, more people arose and sent their greetings to the East until, as the round rim of the Sun edged its way over the horizon, all stopped to face the light and sing greeting to the new day.

A moment later, an ancient man stumbled into the village, his breath coming in harsh gasps. His body was thin and emaciated and his skin was covered with running sores. As he neared one of the lodges, he reached out as if to grasp the woman tending her fire.

"Please Mother," he asked, "give an old man a place to rest and some food to eat so he might grow strong and well."

The woman recoiled from him, shouting, "Go away. Leave us alone. What if my children get your disease? We will all die as you are dying. Go."

The old man waited a moment, but as the woman reached for something to throw at him, he turned and left.

All that day, the old man went from lodge to lodge, asking at each one for food and a place to rest. At each place, he was met with fear, anger, and repulsion. He was turned away from every lodge. Even children had thrown rocks at him. With the day almost gone, there was but one lodge remaining to be approached. It stood apart from the others a little. A small curl of smoke rose from its worn flaps, but the door was open. Inside, an old woman sat mending by her fire. Her hair was white and her face was lined with the tears and laughter of many seasons.

The old woman had not heard the old man approach, so he cleared his throat to let her know he was there. When she looked up, he saw no disgust or fear in her eyes when she beheld him.

"Grandmother," he said. "I am weary and hungry. Please give me a bit of your broth and a place to lie down."

"Come in," the woman said. "There is food and warmth here."

The old man entered and warmed himself while the woman prepared some food. When he had eaten, she gave him a sleeping robe where he slept while she sat mending by the fire.

In the next days, the old man became weaker, in spite of all the woman did to strengthen him and make him comfortable. Finally, the old man said to her, "Grandmother, there is a certain plant which will cure this disease, but I am too weak to go find it. I will teach you the prayer for finding the plant, and will tell you how to recognize it and how to use it. Will you do this?"

The woman agreed, so he told her all she needed to know. She listened to his instructions, made the prayer, and gathered the plant. When she brought the plant back to the lodge, she prepared it according to the old man's instructions and gave it to him.

As the days went by, the old man became stronger, the sores stopped running and began to heal. When he was healthy again, the two old people rejoiced and made prayers of thanks.

In the passing of only a few days, the old man grew sick again. The old woman tended him and did everything she knew to make him better. Nothing gave relief to the new sickness until the old man told the woman of a certain plant that would help him. Once more he told her the right prayer for finding the plant, and gave her instructions for preparing the plant. Again, the woman did as she was told, and when she gave the plant's medicine to the old man he became strong again, and his health was restored.

Again and again the old man became sick, each time with a new disease that the woman could not help. Each time, the old man would tell the woman of the plant and the prayer that would help him. Each time, the woman did as she was instructed, and was able to bring strength and health back again. Many times the old man became ill, and the woman would bring the cure to him, and at times the woman felt she would drop from her tiredness. The work was unending, and the woman sometimes wondered how such a sick old man could remain alive. She continued doing all she was told, and each time, the old man got better.

Finally spring came. One day, the old man said to the woman,

"Grandmother, I must leave soon, but there are things I must tell you first.

"Some time ago, Gitche Manitou looked down upon Creation and saw the people suffering from disease, not knowing how to use the plants that were here to heal every disease. He also saw that the bear knew about these plants that were needed to help the suffering of humans. He gave me a disease and sent me out to find among humans one person with compassion who would give me food and a place by a fire, and learn the ways to heal many sicknesses. He said I would find you, and that you would learn to heal me of all the diseases of mankind. Now that you have learned all these things, you have become one of my clan.

"That is the way it went. You have healed every disease, and you are Bear Clan. It is good. You are a healer and you will teach others who are worthy. You will test them as I have tested you. Gitche Manitou said so. And now I must leave. Farewell."

The old man got up and ambled away. At the edge of the forest, he paused. As the woman looked at him, he became a magnificent black bear. A moment later, he disappeared into the trees.

Ever since that time, the Bear Clan has been known as the Medicine Clan.

—retold by Sun Bear from an old Ojibwa legend

The Legend of Siwash Rock

In the days before the white man came, a woman of the Northern Squamish people came to her husband and said, "Come. It is almost time."

Taking him by the hand, she led him out of the village through giant cedar, fir, spruce, and balsam groves until they came to the shore. After a short time of following the curling beach line they came to a jutting peninsula, and it was at the furthest tip of this that she said, "Here," and turned to make her way into the heavy bushes marking the borderline between beach and forest. He watched her figure, clumsy with child, disappearing and smiled to himself.

"Will it be a boy or a girl?" he wondered softly, then, turning, he waded into the sea and lifted his arms to the sky.

"Great Spirit," he prayed, "cleanse my soul as I swim, as the sea shall cleanse my body. Grant that I may greet this new spirit entering the world totally cleansed in spirit and body so that I will not jeopardize his or her future life in this place. O Great Spirit, strengthen my arms as I swim, that they may keep me afloat in my Sister Ocean until the arrival of the young one. O Source of All Life, grant that I may avoid the shame of Unclean Fatherhood. From me the young one will learn of man . . . Great Spirit, help me now to show him a clean, pure spirit, so that he, too, will live his life in a clean way, praising you. Or if it is a girl, let her know the strengths of man so she will live a life of honor, knowing a pure man when she sees one. O Great Spirit, this child's life depends on you, came from you, and will return to you in the end. Help me now to greet him or her in a manner befitting one who has just recently come from your presence."

And so saying, he plunged into the sea.

Hours passed, as the woman on shore and the man in the water each strove in their own way to greet the child's entrance into this world. In the bushes, the woman was riding another kind of sea, the waves of the sea of life sweeping over and through her body, while out in the channel, the man never ceased his tireless strokes against the ocean tide. As the time moved past him, he imagined he could hear faraway drums beating . . . almost like listening to the pounding hearts of the mountains ringing closely round the land by the water. Slowing his pace somewhat, he lifted his head yet higher above the water. Yes, he could hear it now! Not drumbeats, but a faraway distant chanting, almost indistinguishable against the sound of the ocean tirelessly lashing the beach, almost seeming a part of the mountains and forest and sea.

Looking toward shore, he heard a small cry from his woman. The time was near indeed! Praying to himself now, he resumed cleaving the waters.

As he swam, the distant chant drew nearer, and became clearer to his ears. Eventually the ringing song filled the land and echoed from the sky and mountains.

"We are the messengers of the Great Spirit!" he heard. "Let all who hear hide their eyes, for to look on us is death! We are the messengers of the Great Spirit! Let the waters part before us . . . let all in the sea flee from our path. To touch us or the water we have touched is death!"

His heart sank within him. He had heard, from his grandmother, of the three men, giant spirit-people, sent by the Great Spirit on their unknown mission, and their great canoe which had passed this way twice before, long ago. There had once been a youth in the water who had refused to leave their path. He died.

He glanced at the shore again. If he left the water now, his child would be greeted by an unclean father, and in the very beginning of its life, the most important time of all, it would encounter the limitations of disease, those of the body and also those of the spirit, which will manifest as greed, lethargy, thoughtlessness, carelessness . . . all the associates of an unclean spirit. No, he would not burden his child with these. It would be better to die here in the water than to crawl on the shore at the behest of the three gigantic men in their canoe, and jeopardize his child's whole life.

By this time the canoe had come close enough for the men in it to see him as he resolutely swam onward.

"Ho!" cried the nearest, in the prow.

"Ho, mortal! Are you deaf, that you did not hear us warning the people away as we approached? Why are you still in the water?"

He licked his lips and drank a little salt water to moisten his throat, and pointed to the shore.

"My wife lies in the bushes with our first young one," he answered, and even as he pointed, the distant wail of a newborn child floated across the water. "I would not greet my first child unclean," he said. "I would rather die."

As he waited in the water for his death, his mind traveled back over his recent life. How good she had been to him! And his parents and neighbors. They would throw a huge potlatch in his honor, and give away all their possessions. A time of mourning would follow, after which the neighbors would "mysteriously" replace the necessary tools for living in their section of the longhouse. He knew they would miss him, but accept his loss . . .

He was brought out of his reverie by the steersman rising from the stern of the canoe to point his paddle at him.

"Mortal," he said, not unkindly, "you have shown great bravery in daring our wrath for the sake of your new daughter, for she is indeed a girl-child. With your bravery you have won immortality, for whenever your tribesmen pass you by, they shall see, and recall the virtues of clean fatherhood. You shall pass the ages as a large rock, standing here in the waters where you have defied us, but you shall not be barren, as is one who is forsaken by the Spirit. No, you shall bear three trees, one for each of your loves . . . your wife, your child, and your people."

And extending his paddle, he reached out over the water and lightly touched the man of the Squamish people on the shoulder.

Today, Siwash Rock still stands, and the story of the man who defied the spirits for the sake of his wife and child is still told.

Indeed, the Indians say that if you go to Vancouver, British Columbia, and follow the shore to the furthest tip of Stanley Park, where you can see the bold, beautiful rock holding its hardy trees aloft, you can turn into the underbrush at that point, and if you are lucky, you will find a fairly large rock, about the size of a woman, half-sitting, half-curled on the ground.

Next to it, they say, will be another small rock, in shape vaguely similar to a young newborn baby . . . a lasting tribute to one man's bravery, and forever a reminder to the Squamish peoples to greet their children into this world clean in heart, mind, and body, and so to provide them with a foundation of rocklike strength on which to build their lives.

—retold by Yarrow

How Butterflies Learned to Fly

When the earth was young, there were no butterflies to fly by and brighten the spring and summer days with their wings carrying some of the colors of the rainbow. There were crawlers who were the ancestors of butterflies, but they didn't know how to fly and they would just crawl along the earth. These crawlers were beautiful to see, but all too often people wouldn't watch the earth as they walked and so they missed observing their beauty.

In these days, there was a young woman named Spring Flower, and she was a delight to all who knew her. She always had a smile and a kind word, and her hands felt like the coldest spring to those who were sick with fevers or burns. She would lay her hands upon them, and the fever would leave their body. When she reached the time of womanhood her power became even stronger and, after her vision, she was capable of healing people from most of the sicknesses they could have in those days.

In her vision, strange and beautiful flying creatures had come to her and given her the power of the rainbow that they carried with them. Each color of the rainbow had a special quality of healing that these flyers revealed to her. They told her that, during her life, she would be able to heal and, at the time of her death, she would release healing powers into the air that would stay with the people for all times. The name given to her in her vision was She Who Weaves Rainbows in the Air.

As She Who Weaves Rainbows in the Air grew older, she continued her healing work and her kindness to all whom she met. She also met a man, a dreamer, and took him as her husband. They had two children together and raised them to be strong, healthy, and happy. The two children also had some of the powers of their parents and, later in life, became healers and dreamers themselves.

As She Who Weaves Rainbows in the Air became older her power increased even more, and people from all around the area where she lived came to her with their sick ones, asking her to try to heal them. Those that she could help she helped.

Eventually, the effort of letting all the power come through her made her tired, and she knew that the time to fulfill the other part of her vision drew near. During her life she had noticed that beautifully colored crawlers always came near to her when she sat on the earth. They would come close to her hand and try to rub themselves against it. Sometimes one would crawl up her arm and perch near her ear.

One day when she was resting such a crawler came by her ear. She spoke to it, asking it to tell her what she could do to be of service, as she noticed that it and its brothers and sisters had always been of service to her.

"Sister," said the crawling one, "my people have always been there when you have been healing, helping to bring the colors of the rainbow to you through the colors we wear on our bodies. Now that you are passing into the world of spirit, we don't know how we can continue to bring the healing of these colors to the people. We are earthbound, and the people rarely look down so that they can see us. We feel that if we could fly, the people would notice us and smile at the beautiful colors they see. And we could fly around those who need healing and let the powers of our colors give them whatever healing they can accept. Can you help us to fly?"

She Who Weaves Rainbows in the Air promised to try. She told her husband of her conversation and asked him if any messages might come to him in his dreams.

The next morning he woke up, excited from the dream he had had. When he gently touched She Who Weaves Rainbows in the Air to tell her of it, she did not respond. He sat up and looked closely and saw that his wife had passed into the spirit world during that night.

Through the time of praying for her soul and making preparations for the burial, he remembered that dream that he had had. It comforted him. When it was time to take She Who Weaves Rainbows in the Air to the grove where she would be buried, he looked on her bedding, and waiting for him was the crawler he had expected to find. He gently lifted it up and took it with him.

As they put his wife's body into the earth and prepared to place the soil over her, he heard the crawler say, "Put me on her shoulder now. When the earth is over us my body, too, will die, but my spirit will merge with the spirit of the one who was your wife and together we will fly out of the earth. Then we will go back to my people and teach them how to fly so that the work your wife began can continue. She is waiting for me to come. Put me there now."

The man did as the crawler told him to do, and the burial

proceeded. When all the others had left, the man stayed behind for a while. He looked at the grave, remembering all the love he had had. Suddenly from the grave came a flying one with all the colors of the rainbow spread over its wings. It flew to him and landed on his shoulder.

"Do not be sad, my husband. Now my vision is totally fulfilled, and those who I'll help to teach now will always bring goodness, healing, and happiness to the people. When your time comes to pass into spirit, I'll be waiting to rejoin you."

When the man did change worlds, several years later, and was buried, his children stayed behind after all of the others had gone. They noticed a beautiful one of the new creatures they called butterflies hovering near the grave. In a few minutes, another butterfly of equal beauty flew up and out of their father's grave and joined the one who was waiting and, together, they flew to the North, the place of renewal.

From that time on, butterflies have always been with the people, brightening the air, and our lives, with their beauty.

—from *The Medicine Wheel: Earth Astrology*

Other Recommended Sun Bear Titles

The Path of Power by Sun Bear, Wabun, and Barry Weinstock. Sun Bear's life and lessons are told subtly through stories of his experiences, including the founding and growth of the Bear Tribe. Through his teachings, readers can discover how to accomplish their goals, survive this time of earth cleansing, and follow their own path of power in life.

The Book of the Vision Quest by Steven Foster with Meredith Little. The Vision Quest, a ceremony culminating in a one-day and one-night fast alone in a place of natural power, re-creates an ancient rite of dying, passing through, and being reborn. This book relates the author's experiences in guiding contemporary seekers in the wilderness rite of passage to the vision of themselves and a transformation of love for others and the land.

The Medicine Wheel: Earth Astrology by Sun Bear and Wabun. Sun Bear and his medicine helper, Wabun, set forth a whole new system of earth astrology to help guide people not only in their daily living but in their life path as well. A beautiful and inspiring new approach to astrology, *The Medicine Wheel* will help people of all earth signs walk in balance on our Earth Mother.

For more information about the Bear Tribe and its programs or publications, please write to:

> The Bear Tribe
> P.O. Box 9167
> Spokane, WA 99209-9167

Please enclose a stamped, self-addressed envelope if you wish to have a reply.